EMIRATES
CABIN CREW
JUMP START GUIDE

The complete interview blueprint
and workbook

LAUREN MILLER

The Cabin Crew AirCademy

The Cabin Crew Aircademy presents

EMIRATES CABIN CREW JUMP START GUIDE

Sixth Edition by Lauren Miller

ISBN: 978-1-908300-36-2

Printed in the United Kingdom
10 9 8 7 6 5 4 3 2 1

Library of Congress Cataloging-in-Publication Data

IN ASSOCIATION WITH THE
AIRLINE CAREER INSTITUTE

EMIRATES
CABIN CREW
JUMP START GUIDE

The complete interview blueprint
and workbook

DISCLAIMER

This book is designed to provide information and guidance on attending a cabin crew assessment. It is sold with the understanding that the author is not engaged in rendering legal or other professional services. Such topics, as discussed herein are for example or illustrative purposes only. If expert assistance is required the services of a competent professional should be sought where you can explore the unique aspects of your situation and can receive specific advice tailored to your circumstances.

It is not the purpose of this guide to reprint all the information that is otherwise available but instead to complement, amplify and supplement other texts. You are urged to read all the available material, learn as much as possible about the role and interview techniques and tailor the information to your individual needs.

Every effort has been made to make this guide as complete and accurate as possible, however, this guide contains information that is current only up to the printing date. Interview processes are frequently updated and are often subject to differing interpretations, therefore, there are no absolutes and this text should be used only as a general guide and not as the ultimate source of information.

All information in this book is offered as an opinion of the author and should be taken as such and used with discretion by the reader. You are solely responsible for your use of this book. Neither the publisher nor the author explicitly or implicitly promises that readers will find employment because of anything written or implied here.

The purpose of this guide is to educate and inform. The author shall have neither liability nor responsibility to you or anyone else because of any information contained in or left out of this book.

The views and opinions expressed within this guide are those of the author and do not represent the views of any of Emirates Airlines.

This book is neither associated, approved, affiliated with, nor endorsed by Emirates Airlines.

WELCOME

Hello and welcome to

The Emirates Cabin Crew Jump Start Guide

It's great to have you here and I'm so pleased to be part of your journey. I'm also super excited for you, because you have now taken the first step to realising your dream of becoming cabin crew. Woo hoo.

Now, are you ready to bag yourself the job?
Great. Then let's get started

It's time for your career to take flight...

**Don't forget to claim your FREE bonuses by visiting
www.cabincrewaircademy.com/bonus**

CONTENTS

5 STEPS TO SUCCESS

This book is all about action and, within the following pages, you will find a clear and effective blueprint to follow - a blueprint that will take you through the entire interview process in a 5 step sequence.

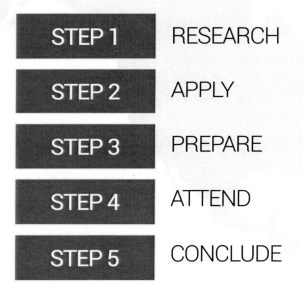

STEP 1	RESEARCH
STEP 2	APPLY
STEP 3	PREPARE
STEP 4	ATTEND
STEP 5	CONCLUDE

Each aspect of the application and selection process is covered in detail, right through to the conclusion.

GETTING STARTED

There are two ways you could work thorugh this course for maximum return on your investment:

Step by Step

If you have the time or are new to the cabin crew recruitment process , I recommend working through each section in the order they are presented, completing each task as you progress.

Since there are some areas that are easily overlooked, this will give you the most bang for your buck, ensuring you have all the information you need and are fully prepared..

Dip in & Dip out

Short on time? Then feel free to dip in and out as needed. This approach also works well if you have specific areas of concern that you want to address directly.

How much time do you need?

Naturally, the more time you can put into this course, the more you will get out of it, however, the goal isn't to make you an interview expert (heck that's my job). The goal is to get you out there living your dream, and in the shortest time possible.

So, only you can be the judge of how much time is needed. This may be as little as one week, or it could be as much as 60 days.

But, if you take action, **you will get results.**

KEY TAKEAWAYS

#1 Schedule it

Schedule an hour a day (or several hour chunks throughout the week) to go through the modules. Make yourself, your career and this course a priority. You'll be thankful you did.

#2 Commit to taking action

I've compiled the data for you, so all you need to do is take action. **You've got this !!!**

QUICK START

Ideally you should allow one month or more to prepare. This will allow you ample time to study the material thoroughly, and apply the strategies without feeling too rushed.

However, it's not always the case that you will have this luxury of time. So, what's the best way to prepare when you only have a matter of weeks, or less?

Step #1 Prepare your application materials

Photographs are a requirement for most airlines, so you should have these readily available.

Although you will be filling out an application form, I highly recommend drafting up your CV as well. This will help you fill out your application form and give you a clear breakdown of your history to refer to.

Step #2 Read what's relevant to your circumstances

If you struggle with any element in particular, maybe your confidence holds you back or you struggle to form cohesive answers, put effort into developing those areas.

STEP #3 Gather facts about the airline

When you are rushed for time, it is tempting to skip the research section of this course, however, it would be a cardinal sin to arrive at the interview without having at least a basic knowledge of Emirates operations. Having background knowledge about Emirates will show that you are enthusiastic and prepared. A quality often desired in cabin crew.

STEP #4 : Prepare for potential questions

At the very least, you should be prepared to answer questions such as:

» Why do you want to become cabin crew?
» Why do you want to work for us?
» Why should we hire you?
» What are your weaknesses?

Also be sure to gather a selection of examples which demonstrate your customer service and teamworking experience., particularly those of an adverse nature.

STEP #5 : Prepare a list of questions

Having intelligent questions prepared for the recruiters will set you apart as a prepared and enthusiastic candidate.

STEP #6 : Rehearse

Rehearsing the interview process under simulated conditions will highlight potential areas of weakness. This will give you a better idea of where to focus your time and energy.

STEP #7 : Prepare your outfit

This may seem obvious, but you'd be surprised how many people leave this step until the morning of the interview only to find that they don't have anything appropriate to wear, or have stains on their attire. Your groomng is important for the cabin crew role, so make a good impression by planning your attire ahead of time.

STEP #8

Do the best you can

Once you have all the above steps completed, try to get as much reading in as possible. The average reading speed is said to be 150-250 words per minute. This means that, even at the slower pace of 150 words, you'll be able to get through much of the content with a few hours set aside. Do the best you can.

Remember, if you don't sacrifice for what you want, what you want becomes the sacrifice, so put your all into making this a success and you'll reap the rewards.

STEP #9

Believe in yourself

When you have been through a few cabin crew interview experiences, it is easy to feel overwhelmed by the process, but I assure you that it's not complicated or tricky. All you need is some guidance and strategies, and that's what I will provide you with in this step by step blueprint. It's time to realise your cabin crew dreams.

"

Choose a career you *love* and you will never work a day in your life

Dare to dream

INTRO

THE ROLE
OF CABIN CREW

Cabin crew are on board an aircraft primarily for safety reasons. In the event of a real life emergency, the cabin crew must ensure that passengers follow the captains instructions, use safety equipment correctly and stay as calm as possible.

During the course of a flight, your responsibilities will be as diverse as the needs of the customers so you will need to be prepared for the unexpected however; here's a quick rundown of the type of things you can expect to be doing:

You will spend a lot of time attending to essential needs such as looking after the comfort and wellbeing of passengers. This will involve providing a meal service, providing advice, sympathy and reassurance, ensuring passenger safety, engaging customers in conversation, and giving special attention to disabled, people who are ill or children travelling alone.

There will also be paperwork to complete, this can include flight reports, customs and immigration documents, accounts of duty free sales and meal and drink orders.

Overall, you will be expected to deliver the highest standards of customer service so you will need to go the extra mile for each and every passenger and be sure that everything, within reason, is possible.

AB-INITIO
TRAINING

Emirates provide an intensive six-week crew training course for newcomers. The training is held at the Emirates Aviation College in Dubai and is conducted in English.

The training course is an intense course and you will need to allow plenty of time for revision outside the classroom. At the same time, it is very rewarding and is delivered in a fun and informative way.

The training includes practical and theoretical aspects of cabin service and uniform standards, cultural awareness and customer service, product knowledge, safety equipment and procedures, aircraft checks and documentation, aviation security and dangerous goods, first aid, and assertiveness training.

To graduate from training as Emirates cabin crew, you will need to pass regular assessments on all subjects studied on the course.

Each module has stringent pass marks; hence a high standard of performance and dedication is required. In the event of exam failure, you are permitted one re-sit. Alternatively, you will be given the opportunity to go back one week which would entail joining another training group. A subsequent failure of an exam would have to result in withdrawal from the course.

On graduation from the course, you will have the confidence to deal with any situation onboard an aircraft and be able to deliver the unique Emirates service.

The first six months of flying duties are seen as a continuation of this initial training thus you will receive further on-board training and assessments.

A salary advance and company accommodation is provided during training.

ADVANCEMENT
OPPORTUNITIES

There are amazing career advancement opportunities within Emirates and certainly far more rapid and attainable than what you would find with other airlines.

Currently high performing Cabin Crew have been able to attain the position of flight purser within five years and have also opportunities to become trainers on cabin service.

There are many people in mid and upper management who started with the company as Cabin Crew and now work in various other departments.

A network of learning resource centres exist in various Emirates group buildings in Dubai. They provide an environment for self or group-based study. They provide access to online and CD Rom based courses, all available at flexible times to suit employee schedules.

LIFE IN DUBAI

Situated on the northeast coast of the United Arab Emirates (UAE), the Emirate of Dubai shares borders with Abu Dhabi, Sharjah and the Sultanate of Oman.

Dubai is the second largest of 7 Emirates that make up the UAE and occupies around 3,900 square kilometres.

The population of Dubai is estimated at around 1,204,000 people and is made up of more than 130 nationalities - bringing a richly cosmopolitan character to the city.

Arabic is the national language, however, English, Urdu, Hindi and Farsi are spoken widely. Arabic and English are the main business languages.

Dubai has a sub-tropical and arid climate, with sunny blue skies most of the year. It rains infrequently, falling mainly in winter. Temperatures range from a low of about 10.5°C (50°F) to a high of 48°C (118°F). The mean daily maximum in January is 24°C/75.2°F rising to 41°C/105.8°F in July with high humidity levels.

The monetary unit in the UAE is the Dirham (Dhs/ AED) which is divided into 100 fils. It has been held constant against the US dollar since the end of 1980 at a mid-rate of approximately US$1= Dh3.66.

In 2003, Dubai was voted the safest holiday destination in the world by leading travel magazine Conde Nast Traveller - Dubai bagged the award for the second year in a row.

Living in Dubai you will find that it is virtually crime-free with the Dubai police ensuring personal safety and security.

Dubai's culture is firmly rooted in the traditions of Islam and traditional dress is still worn among many local citizens. However, Dubai is a very tolerant and welcoming place for foreigners, with visitors free to follow their own religions.

The dress code is liberal for visitors and women are allowed to drive and go out unescorted.

Dubai offers a multitude of attractions for visitors, from miles of beautiful white sandy beaches, towering sand dunes, barren Rocky Mountains, PGA-standard golf courses, brand new shopping malls, ancient Arabic forts and lively international bars, restaurants and nightclubs.

Dubai's restaurants provide cuisine of every nationality possible, ranging from typical Arabic food, European, Indian to Far Eastern and American - the list is endless. Whether it's fine dining or fast food you want, Dubai has an outstanding choice of restaurants to choose from. There are numerous international fast food chains such as McDonalds, Burger King, Hardees's, Kentucky Fried Chicken, Pizza Hut, Round Table Pizza and Pizza Corner. Theme restaurants such as TGI Friday's, Planet Hollywood, Hard Rock Café and Henry J Bean's can also be found around the city. Only restaurants in hotels and leisure complexes are licensed to sell alcoholic beverages.

Dubai has earned an international reputation as the shopping capital of the Middle East. And indeed you will find some of the best duty free shopping in the world in this city, including jewellery, clothing, unique local items, art and much more. The annual Dubai Shopping Festival extravaganza has rapidly become an internationally-known event. It is a city of contrasts; you can be assured of an exciting pace of life in Dubai and a high standard of living.

OVERVIEW
OF THE SELECTION PROCESS

If you are aspiring to be part of the prestigious Emirates cabin crew team, I have devised this concise step by step walkthrough so that you can anticipate and prepare for the process that lies ahead.

Over recent months, Emirates have been giving their recruitment process an overhaul. In November 2016, Emirates announced they would no longer be holding open days, and all new applications will need to be filed through the Emirates Group Careers Website. In addition, Emirates have also introduced a pre-recorded video interview as part of the application process. Because of these ongoing updates to the process, the following outline is only a guide for what you can expect and is subject to change.

Here's the good news

If you have ever attended an Emirates open day, you'll know that they were more like cattle calls as they would attract an extremely large turnout of candidates. Here are some of the quoted figures:

+ Almost 400 people turned out at a 2010 open day in Madrid
+ 1200 people turned up to a 2006 open day in Cairo
+ Another 1000 attended a 2008 open day in Fiji
+ and each recruitment drive generally attracted over 1000 people in Thailand

Read more by visiting: Sky's The Limit (http://www.theemiratesgroup.com/english/news-events/news-releases/news-details.aspx?article=545294

With so many candidates turning up at any one event, the process was a long and arduous one for both the candidates and recruiters alike. The elimination of these open days and the introduction of video interviews will no doubt make future assessment days with Emirates much more reasonable in size because only those candidates who have been shortlisted will be invited to attend. Better yet, this streamlined process will make it much more likely that you'll be successful for the following reasons

1. Fewer candidates means that it will be easier to stand out
2. In being invited to participate, it means you've already passed the initial pre-screening and have made a positive impression

And the better news...

Believe it or not, having the opportunity to do a video interview will make the process easier to prepare for.

If you are a little self conscious of speaking in front of a camera, I understand that the concept may be difficult to grasp at first, but it's true. Think about it like this, when you attend a live interview, you get one chance to say and do the right thing. With a video, you can practice and prepare as much as you need before you sit down to do the recording. There are many second chances to get it right.

In fact, the video interview can make you a better candidate overall because you'll begin to pick up on nuances in your voice, answers and behaviour that you wouldn't have otherwise, and you'll be able to correct and perfect along the way.

Anyway, I'm getting ahead of myself, we'll get back to tips for the video interview later.

Emphasis on pre-screening

With the emphasis being placed on pre-screening candidates, it's more important than ever to have a powerful resume and online presence to match.

Below you'll find a detailed outline taking you from the initial application, all the way through to the final interview, and everything in between.

As noted previously, be aware of changes as the new processes are rolled out and use this information as a guide only.

On a side note, I just want to reiterate that the process of getting a cabin crew position is only as hard as you make it. Please forget what others have told you, forget what may have happened in the past and start over with a fresh perspective. A perspective that is backed by new research and preparation.

The only thing standing in your way is you, so get out of your own way, believe in yourself and live your dream. You can do this.

STEP ONE
SUBMIT THE ONLINE APPLICATION

Applications for cabin crew can be submitted via the official Emirates Group Careers Website.

If no positions are open when you visit the site, your best bet is to follow Emirates on their LinkedIn Profile so that you receive up to date alerts. At the time of writing this post, Emirates have seized recruitment for some time, so head on over to LinkedIn and get in the loop. Alternatively, you can follow The Cabin Crew Aircademy On Facebook and you'll receive updates and walkthroughs as they are made available.

If you would like assistance with these sections, please refer back to the previous module that cover the Emirates application process.

STEP TWO
COMPLETE A VIDEO INTERVIEW

As part of your online application, you'll need to participate in a video interview.

The video interview is super duper simple to complete, even if you don't like recording videos, this system is so streamlined you'll find it a breeze.

You'll be asked up to 5 short questions, each very simple in nature. You'll be given 30 seconds to prepare for each recording and a full minute to record your response. Both are timed and you can press the button to begin and end your recording.

To help you set up, there is a video viewing window that you can use to adjust your position and make yourself look all pretty before you recrod, but you also have the option to hide the video recording from your view if you find this intimidating.

In a real interview, you'll not be given 30 seconds to prepare your answer, so this is a great opportunity to shine. Give it all you got and demonstrate your enthusiasm.

The interview is very short and you can expect anywhere up to 5 minutes for the answers themselves, plus your preparation time. Make sure you put a clear 20 minutes aside where you won't be interrupted.

You'll need to take the video screening very seriously because you'll not be invited along to an assessment day if you don't pass this section of the process. I can't emphasise enough that you should prepare as if you are attending the final interview.

A few tips that have helped me to pass this part of the process are:

✈ Dress as if you are attending the interview
✈ Keep some notes handy that you can easily refer to
✈ Relax and approach the video as if you are speaking to a friend.
✈ Be sure to have your computer plugged in to avoid battery depletion
✈ Close any apps that may pop up
✈ Practice, practice again and then again.

Questions that have been asked previously include:

✈ Can you give an example of a time when you exceeded a customers expectations?
✈ Why do you want to be Cabin Crew?
✈ Why do you want to work for Emirates?
✈ What planes do we have in our fleet and what destinations do we fly to?
✈ How would you wow a customer?
✈ What do you know about Dubai and the Muslim culture?
✈ What do you do in your spare time?

I have devised a thorough section on acing the video interview in a later section, please refer to this for more guidance.

STEP THREE
ATTEND THE ASSESSMENT DAY

Prior the the 2017 updates, the Emirates assessment day was broken down into the following stages:

✈ Orientation and video presentation
✈ English test
✈ Height & reach test
✈ Group discussions
✈ Final Interview

Typically the final interview was scheduled for the day after or a mutually convenient time at a later date. With the new and streamlined recruitment process, it is possible that final interviews will be held on the same day, but this is yet to be confirmed as the new process is rolled out.

Orientation and video presentation

During the orientation, the recruitment officers would play a short video presentation of the airline, then briefly go over the role of cabin crew, the benefits of the position, Dubai and it's culture, and some facts about Emirates. Candidates will be given the opportunity to ask questions during this stage, and it is a great opportunity to stand out and demonstrate your research if you can do so with confidence.

> **Pro tip:** Be sure that whatever question you ask at this stage has not already been answered in the literature, and never ask questions related to the benefits of the job. Ask about the culture in Dubai, the transition to living within a Muslim country, and facts related to the airline, but avoid overly complex questions that require a lot of explanation. This part of the assessment is not meant to be long winded or in depth. You'll have plenty of time to ask more detailed questions during the final interview, and you never want the recruiters to decline to answer due to the length of time needed to respond. Keep things simple.

English Test

Going by the variety of experiences reported back and that of my own, it would appear that the English test comes in a variety of different forms and may change. The test I remember was split into two parts:

✈ Reading comprehension
✈ Writing task

The reading comprehension part consisted of reading a piece of text and then answering questions about the text through a series of multiple choice answers.

The written part of the assessment was to write an answer to the question "What do you think the role of cabin crew involves?". Other questions that have been asked are: "Name three things about yourself that you want to improve" and "Describe an experience when you satisfied a customer".

Pro tip: As you may be able to gather from the questions asked, this assessment is about more than your ability to understand English. Your answer is an opportunity to demonstrate your knowledge and suitability for the position. Take some time to think about your answer, and be sure to put extra effort into writing clearly with good use of grammar and spelling. Your level of English doesn't have to be to academic standards, but it should be to a high level.

Height and Reach Test (and grooming standards)

In order to progress onto the group discussions, you are assessed against the height and reach requirements. At the time of writing, the reach requirement is 212cm on tip toes. You will be asked to remove your shoes and I'd also suggest removing your jacket to avoid any potential constraints in your reach. This test is strict and anyone not able to reach the required level are asked to leave at this point. To date, the Emirates test has been a simple vertical reach and height test, but this could of course change.

As part of this assessment you'll also be asked if you have any tattoos. The image below represents the areas that are considered off limits, and this applies to most airlines. Any tattoos beyond the blue regions will be visible while in uniform, so if you have tattoos in any of these areas you will be asked to leave at this point. Cover up is not an option.

This also applies if you have any tattoos under your hair, for instance on your neck or behind your ears. The policy on tattoos is very strict, and not just with Emirates. There are no exceptions.

Group Discussions

With the preliminary assessments complete, the remaining candidates are split into groups for the discussions. There tends to be 2 discussion rounds, followed by a short break and elimination round, then followed up with a further 2 discussion rounds to finish the process. The discussions come in a variety of topics, including, but not limited to current affairs and hypothetical scenarios. Some of the discussions that have come up in the past are:

✈ Discuss your thoughts regarding the ban on public smoking
✈ There is only one room left in the hotel, but you have a party of 7 guests. Who should have the room?
✈ The plane has gone down over the Atlantic. Only one life raft remains with the ability to hold 5 people, but 7 survivors remain. Who should be saved and why?
✈ You have been asked to entertain 5 children for the day. These children have disabilities. Where would you take them and why?

Pro tip: During the group discussions, it's typical for the most extroverted candidates to jump right in. This is the most challenging part of the whole process because everyone wants to stand out and will fight to achieve it leaving many candidates at the wayside struggling to get involved. I've seen arguments erupt when things have got so heated. A small heads up, that's not a good way to go through to the next round.

If you are an extroverted type, resist the temptation to get carried away. Disagreeing is fine when done constructively, but this is a group assessment, and that means working as a team to collaborate and discuss ideas. Candidates who don't consider others are not viewed favourably and are often eliminated. As long as you get involved and are positive throughout the interaction, you will be noticed. There's no need to be the centre of attention. In fact, the best way to use your extroverted side is to assist other candidates if you see they are struggling to get involved.

On the other hand, if you have introverted tendencies or are on the quieter side, you will need to come out of your comfort zone in order to get involved. This can be difficult when a discussion is in full flow, but it is absolutely necessary if you are to progress through the rounds. No involvement means the recruiters have nothing to assess, so get involved however you can even if only briefly.

Interesting Point: I am one of those quieter individuals and struggled with this for many years. I remember during the first round of group discussions, the task was nearing it's conclusion and I realised I hadn't made a comment. I was fully aware that I wouldn't be going through to the next round if I didn't say something, so as soon as I sensed a split second gap, I proceeded to make one comment. That comment got me through to the next round and I was ultimately successful in the being offered the position. Interestingly, many of the candidates who I went through with were also on the introverted side, so take note that being the life and soul of the party is not always necessary, just as being quiet doesn't automatically eliminate you from the process.

A lot of this has to do with corporate culture and the type of person that Emirates are seeking to employ. *The corporate culture will be addressed in a later section.*

The good news is, after the first round of discussions the assessment will break for 20-30 minutes and another set of eliminations will take place. This drastically reduces the size of the group and further assessments are much more relaxed. If you make it through this first section, the rest of the assessment gets a whole lot easier.

On a final note, the topics or outcomes of the discussions are not what's relevant during these tasks, it's how you interact within a group environment that is under assessment. Be courteous, listen to your peers, relax, smile and have fun.

Variations in the process

This is a basic outline, but some variations have been shown to exist. On my assessment day there was a short one to one with the recruiter and a psychometric test at the end of the day. Other candidates have reported completing a personal presentation round before the group assessments. Variations also seem to exist depending on your country the assessment is undertaken. In the US, the first part of the day appears to be made up of two presentations followed by a role play.

In essence, the best way to prepare is to be prepared for anything.

S T E P ✈ F O U R

STEP FOUR
ATTEND THE FINAL INTERVIEW

By now, you've passed the pre-screening and have impressed the recruitment team during the group assessments, so if you have made it this far you are doing extremely well. The recruiters already like you, and all that's left is to close out the process by telling them a little bit about you and your background.

It really is that simple, so forget the horror stories circulating the internet. Don't make more of this than needed because you'll only work yourself up into a bag of nerves.

The whole purpose of the final interview is to discover your motives for applying and your suitability for the position, that's it.

To date, the final interview has been conducted by 2 recruiters. This usually consists of one asking the questions, and the other observing.

In terms of length, this varies dramatically. Some report an hour, while others report just 30 minutes. It's unlikely that the interview will go on longer than an hour, so be prepared for an hour and anything less will be a bonus.

My final interview was so short that I left feeling stunned. Only 20 minutes into the interview and it was over. Talk about confusion. I didn't know how to take that, whether it was a good sign or a bad sign.

The Questions

The interview tends to get underway with a few traditional icebreaker questions. For instance, you can expect the following:

✈ Tell me a little bit about yourself
✈ Why do you want to be cabin crew?
✈ Why do you want to work for Emirates?
✈ What do you know about Emirates?
✈ What do you know and understand about the lifestyle in Dubai?
✈ How do you feel about relocating to Dubai?
✈ Describe three cultural differences you've experienced while traveling?

After these, the questions will turn exclusively to behavioural based scenarios.

Behavioural questions, also referred to as competency based, are all experience related. You can expect a variety of these types of questions, each looking to determine your level of competency related to the responsibilities of cabin crew, such as teamwork, customer service, and your ability to work under pressure. Here are some example questions:

- ✈ Tell me about a time when you went out of your way for a customer
- ✈ When have you had to deal with a customer complaint
- ✈ Describe an experience of working as part of a team
- ✈ Tell me about a time when you received an unsatisfactory service as a customer
- ✈ Describe a time when you needed to be assertive
- ✈ Give me an example of a time when you had to lead

Ask your own questions

At the end of the interview, you'll be given the opportunity to ask any questions you have. If you haven't already answered questions related to your knowledge of Dubai or Emirates, or if there's something specific that hasn't been covered, ask your questions here.

I remember asking the recruiter how she found the transition to living in a Muslim country and what it was like during the holy month of Ramadan. Her eyes lit up and I knew I'd asked the right question.

When you ask intelligent questions, it stands out. Getting a cabin crew job with Emirates is not just a simple career move, it's a whole new lifestyle. What questions could you ask that will show you are thinking logically and intelligently about this transition?A salary advance and company accommodation is provided during training.

STEP FIVE
COMPLETE A PERSONALITY TEST

The personality test is based on a simple rating scale and is very easy to complete.

Ratings are generally a sliding scale as follows:

✈ Strongly disagree
✈ Disagree
✈ Neutral
✈ Agree
✈ Strongly agree

Some examples of the type of questions on these test are:

- ✈ When making a decision, you rely more on your feelings than on analysis of the situation
- ✈ You prefer to act immediately rather than speculate about various options
- ✈ You trust reason rather than feelings
- ✈ You are inclined to rely more on improvisation than on prior planning
- ✈ I make friends easily
- ✈ I feel comfortable around new people

My Experience: When I completed the personality test, it was given out and completed as part of the group assessment. Somewhere along the process, I had missed a box. As I was nearing the end of the test, the boxes didn't match up and I realised my error. My form ended up being a bit of a mess as I had to cross through a third of my answers and correct the entries. Thankfully it was at the end of the assessments and I had already made a good impression, so this seemed to be overlooked. Needless to say, I was very lucky this didn't ruin everything I had worked for.

These tests really are quite easy to complete, and all that's required is a little forethought and judgement.

STEP SIX
DISCOVER YOUR OUTCOME

After the final interview is complete, your file will be sent on to the Dubai Head Office for assessment and final approval.

This process can take some time because your file will need to be manually reviewed. I waited several weeks before receiving the golden call. Having said that, the process was extended for me before of a mix up with my final interview date and the fact that I had to submit four sets of photos before they were accepted.

If you are one of the selected candidates, you'll receive confirmation an email to confirm the offer of employment along with a phone call from Dubai HR, aka the "**Golden Call**".

Ref: ▓▓▓▓▓▓▓

Ms. ▓▓▓▓▓▓▓▓▓▓
Birmingham
England

Dear Ms. ▓▓▓▓

I am pleased to offer you employment with **Emirates** as Stewarde▓
Department, with a commencement date of **28-Jul-2005**.

Your Contract of Employment with the Company will be for a peri▓
commencement date. Thereafter, your contract will be reviewed b▓
renewed on mutual agreement but without any obligation on the Compa▓

The terms and conditions of your employment with the Company are▓
Employment Regulations Manual, the Pay and Allowances Manual, an▓
which relate to your job and which will be available to you when ▓
"Cabin Crew Handbook" contains further relev▓▓▓▓▓▓▓
6 of the Emirates Group ▓▓▓▓▓▓

PART ONE
RESEARCH

RESEARCH
THE REQUIREMENTS

As you may be aware, this is the airline I worked for once upon a time, so Emirates hold a very special place in my heart and I can relate to your desire to work for such an incredible airline.

You've made a great choice, and I hope I can turn my knowledge and experience into helping you with your own success.

So, let's proceed.

In order to qualify for a cabin crew position with Emirates, you'll need to satisfy the **eligibility**, **suitability** and **specific requirements**.

In addition to those requirements is compatibility with Emirates corporate culture.

This section will explore each of these in detail. We will cover

✈ The Emirates Corporate Culture
✈ Minimum Requirements to Apply

ACTION STEP
Emirates include a very detailed breakdown of their requirements on their website so head on over to the Emirates Career Site and have a quick browse through to familiarise yourself with the basics.

THE REQUIREMENTS

The requirements to become Emirates Cabin Crew are quite a lot different from other airlines. Besides the requirement to relocate to Dubai, you'll also need to be at least 21 years old. While the age requirement is higher than most other airlines, Emirates do have a relaxed approach to other areas that others may be stricter with, such as the ability to swim.

Here is the complete list of requirements you'll need to meet to qualify for the position with Emirates

WHAT YOU'LL NEED

There are a few qualities which will make you stand out. Namely, you'll be positive, confident, flexible, friendly and very keen to help others. Here are the other things we look for in our candidates.

- At least 21 years of age at the time of joining
- Arm reach of 212 cm while standing on tiptoes
- Minimum height of 160 cm
- High school graduate (Grade 12)
- Fluency in English (written and spoken)
- No visible tattoos while you're in Emirates cabin crew uniform (cosmetic and bandage coverings aren't allowed)
- Can adapt to new people, new places and new situations
- Physically fit for this demanding role

(Source: Emirates Careers Website)

SWIMMING

Emirates have a relaxed swimming requirement and actually don't state any specific abilities within their requirements.

If you're not a strong swimmer and are wondering what this means for you, it means that there is NO swimming requirement. Of course this is subject to change in future recruitment drives but, for now at least, you are not required to be able to have any specific swimming abilities.

This is a welcome relief to the normal requirements of being able to tread water and swim the Atlantic ocean – only kidding slightly.

MY EXPERIENCE

Since drowning as a child, I have been afraid of the water. Before applying to Emirates and learning of the no swimming requirement, I faced my fear and taught myself to swim.

During ditching training, the instructors asked if anyone couldn't swim. I didn't want to fail, so I didn't raise my hand and continued to participate.

As it came to my turn, I moved to the edge of the raft, proceeded to climb over and slipped into the water. My mouth filled with water and began to panic. A long story short, the other trainees had to save me from my drowning episode.

After the water training concluded, I passed but was marked down because I hadn't told anyone of my fear of the water. When asked why I had lied, I told the examiner I didn't want to fail and that was when they told me that swimming is not a requirement to pass or fail.

So there you have it, I have tried and tested the theory myself.

RESIDENCY

As you are no doubt aware, you'll also need to be prepared to relocate to Dubai, UAE. For most of you this is the attraction of the job, for others this may be a challenge.

The good news is, you'll not need to travel to Dubai for any assessments prior to joining as these will be carried out in your home country before being officially offered the position.

Once the official contracts are in place, pre-employment medicals and reference checks are complete, Emirates will fly you over to Dubai to begin training... And yes, flight costs will be borne by Emirates.

ARE YOU CULTURE FIT?

THE EMIRATES CORPORATE CULTURE

Corporate culture this is an essential, yet often overlooked, requirement.

Corporate culture is a term used to describe the collective attitudes, beliefs, behaviours and values that exist within an organisation. In essence, it is the character of the airline.

Corporate Culture is the foundation of any company, not just airlines, and finding a match for that distinctive culture is of the utmost importance if the airline is going to maintain their unique identity, but also find candidates who will fit in and enjoy the environment day to day. Individuals who don't share in the culture are unlikely to enjoy working within the environment for long.

During your assessment, you will be constantly observed according to this culture and if your personality doesn't appear to fit, it is unlikely you'll be successful in the interview process. So what is the Emirates corporate culture?

ISLAMIC ROOTS AND TRADITIONS

Emirates are a truly cosmopolitan airline hiring crew from around the globe, however it's roots are still firmly grounded in the Islamic culture. The distinctive scarf that cabin crew wear as part of their uniform depicts these roots and Muslim traditions.

Now that Emirates and Dubai are internationally renowned and popularised, it is easy to forget these roots, however, if you are to become cabin crew with Emirates and relocate to Dubai, an understanding and appreciation for this culture is a must because you'll be living and breathing a completely different lifestyle.

Because of your eventual relocation to Dubai, the corporate culture requirements extend beyond the normal boundaries of the airline. If you have ever been to Dubai, you'll understand that Emirates Airline have a massive public presence, so you'll be representing the brand even while out of uniform in your day to day life.

It's not all glam. The way of life you may be used to will need to be adjusted. Everyday things that Western civilisations take for granted, for instance you'll need a licence to purchase alchoholic beverages, living with a partner before marriage is frowned upon, and you could be arreste for being affectionate or wearing certain garments in public.

Because of these changes in lifestyle, your ability and willingness to transition will come into question during your assessment, so be sure to do some background research on Dubai and the culture. In fact, having some knowledge regarding the culture itself can be used as a huge advantage that may set you apart.

When attending your assessment or filing any forms, you'll need to be very mindful of this aspect because it will dictate how you will groom yourself for your assessment, how you will approach the process itself and what answers you provide.

Okay, not that we've covered the heritage, let's get back to the Emirates corporate culture itself.

THE DISTINCTIVE CULTURE

So, as we've established, Emirates have a very distinctive heritage, but what else do they represent?

The best way to determine the corporate culture is to think about the words that conjure up in your mind when you think about the airline.

For Emirates, the words that I would use to describe the airline are:

- ✈ Rich / Wealth
- ✈ Cosmopolitan
- ✈ International
- ✈ Luxurious
- ✈ Prestige

- ✈ Royal
- ✈ Modest / Conservative
- ✈ Diverse
- ✈ Tasteful
- ✈ Prosperity

In addition to these words, the Emirates logo itself gives an insight into what Emirates consider to be important.

It is said that the red colour in the Emirates logo represents **prosperity, self-confidence, passion and leadership.** The white colour depicts **nobility, elegance and purity.**

Can you think of any others? or maybe yours are different to mine. In any case, when considering these words, you get an understanding of how you can best approach your interview in order to be successful. If you can embody those words yourself, you'll be seen as Emirates material.

So, how do you embody those words? Through your appearance, the words you use and the way you conduct yourself.

ACT THE PART

BEHAVE THE PART

One thing that I have seen with Emirates is that the candidates who tend to be successful are usually the ones that don't stand out a great deal. That's because Emirates like modesty.

I remember my own successful assessment day because I was still suffering from anxiety at the time and came across as more shy and introverted. Speaking out back then was a real struggle and I had to force myself to get involved. In hindsight, this worked to my advantage because many of those who I went thorugh to the next round with were also relatively quiet. Conversely, I remember those candidates who took over the discussions were promptly eliminated.

I'm not saying that you should be shy and quiet, because you do need to get involved in order to be assessed.

What makes a candidate successful with Emirates are those candidates who:

✈ Think before they speak
✈ Are modest in their approach
✈ Willing to discuss openly and not take over
✈ Value the opinions of others and help others get involved

Emirates assessments are not about popularity contests or who can get the most airtime with their opinions, it's about coming together as a team and being respectful to each other.

Sounds obvious I know, but it needs emphasising because I've literally seen candidates get into heated arguments during a discussion.

DRESS THE PART

Picking out what to wear is an easy one with Emirates because they have a very specific dress code on their website that you must follow. And when I say must, I really mean that you MUST follow those guidelines. Emirates are very very strict about their requirements and you'll be eliminated if you deviate.

So head on over to the Emirates Career Site and follow their own instructions.

ASSESSMENT DAY DRESS CODE

(Source: Emirates Careers Website)

STAND OUT
AS A TOP APPLICANT

UGH, RESEARCH!!!

I know, boring right. But what if I told you that research is the one aspect that can make or break your chances of success?

Do you know how many people turn up to an interview not knowing a single thing about the airline? Other than it's list of exotic destinations! Well, I can tell you that it's well above 90%, and that's being generous. Do you know what happens to these candidates? They appear unprepared and unenthusiastic, and they get rejected.

This means, If you spend just a small amount of time learning some key facts, you are going to stand out as someone who has taken the time to do their homework. And this my dear friend is exactly the type of person that Emirates are looking to recruit.

With the volume of candidates that apply to Emirates these days, it is becoming more and more likely that you'll be asked to recount your knowledge of the airline. Those who have no real knowledge understandably don't progress very far.

As a secondary benefit, when you conduct background research, your own reasons for wanting to join Emirates will be enhanced. This means that when the recruiter asks you a question such as "Why do you want to work for Emirates?" or "Why should we hire you?" you are going to be armed with facts and solid reasons to justify your response and demonstrate your enthusiasm.

This will achieve the two objectives of this section, which are:

✈ To enable you to effectively demonstrate your fit for the airline
✈ To have you standing out as an informed applicant.

YOU'LL DISCOVER
So here's what you will discover within this module:

✈ Where to look
I will show you some hidden gems that will make your research tasks quick, accurate and up to date.

✈ What to learn
You will learn how much and to what depth is necessary, thereby only learning what is essential and helpful to your candidacy.

WHERE TO LOOK

Social media pages are the first place to check for up to date information that is fresh off the press.

✈ Emirates FaceBook Profile
https://www.facebook.com/Emirates/

✈ Emirates Twitter Profile
https://twitter.com/emirates

For the purposes of recruitment, you'll want to dig a little deeper than the obvious social media profiles.

The best place to get up to date, accurate and comprehensive information about an airline, it's past, present and future, is in it's press pack, also known as a media kit.

The press pack is a comprehensive, yet condensed set of promotional materials that have been put together for members of the media. Essentially, this is the equivalent of a resume but for the airline.

Find Emirates press pack at the following location:

✈ Emirates Media Centre
https://www.emirates.com/media-centre/

And their annual report can be found at:

✈ Emirates Annual Report
https://cdn.ek.aero/downloads/ek/pdfs/report/annual_report_2017.pdf

Another great source for the basic information is Wikipedia, however, the information may not be completely up to date, so it is best consulted for historical facts only.

WHAT'S IN THE PRESS PACK?

A press kit will contains the following elements:

✈ Overview of the airline
✈ Profiles of key people
✈ Route and aircraft information
✈ Important news coverage
✈ Awards and initiatives
✈ Mission, goals & objectives
✈ Alliances

and many more interesting facts and goodies...

WHAT YOU SHOULD LEARN

I've created some detailed cheat sheets for you later in the next sections, but you'll learn best by using your own initiative and conducting your own research, so here are the guidelines to help you get the most out of your research.

You will find there is a tonne of information in these press packs, and you certainly do not need or want to know all of it. So, you will need to sift through and extract just a few key bits and pieces.

Here are some things to look out for:

✈ Who is the key person? (e.g. CEO, founder or chairman)
✈ Is the airline part of an alliance? Or does it have any partnerships?
✈ What are the important growth plans? (1 year, 5 year, long term)
✈ What are three of the most prominent awards? How many have they won? What does the airline pride itself on?
✈ What is the story behind it's incorporation? When did it begin operations?
✈ Which 3 airlines are considered to be the closest major competitors? What are key differences?
✈ What is the frequent flyer programme called?
✈ How many destinations are in their route network? Does it focus on a particular region? Do they have plans to change or add to this?
✈ Is there anything significant about their fleet of aircraft? How many? What type? Does it have plans for updating its fleet?
✈ What is the overall mission of the airline? What is it's tagline?
✈ Is there anything unique or distinctive about this airline?

Although this list may appear overwhelming at rst, you'll be surprised how much of the information you will retain just by extracting and then writing it out in your workbook. The bottom line is, these are all the facts about your dream airline, and future employer. It's worth learning about

CHEAT SHEET
SHORT AND SWEET

THE ESSENTIALS

Slogan: The tagline was changed to "HELLO TOMORROW" in 2012 from its previous tagline "FLY EMIRATES, KEEP DISCOVERING".

IATA: EK

Headquarters: Garhoud, Dubai, United Arab Emirates

Hub: Dubai International Airport (DXB)

Commenced Operations: 25 October 1985.

Annual Passenger Numbers: 56,076 million (2016-2017 up 8.1% from 51,853 million (2015-2016)

Chairman & CEO: His Highness Sheikh Ahmed Bin Saeed Al Maktoum

The Emirates Logo: It is said that the red colour in the Emirates logo represents prosperity, self-confidence, passion and leadership. The white colour depicts nobility, elegance and purity.

Expansion: Emirates became one of the world's largest long haul airlines in just thirty years. According to the Emirates website, the airline adds an average of four new destinations every year and regularly increases flight frequencies. Emirates also continue to expand their fleet, averaging one new aircraft delivery each month. In 2016-17, Emirates added 35 new aircraft to its fleet.

Notable Awards:

World's Best Airline (Skytrax World Airline Awards 2016) This is the fourth time Emirates has won this top prize in the awards history.

World's Best Airline and Best Middle Eastern Airline (ULTRAS 2017)

Best Airline in the World (TripAdvisor Travellers Choice Awards 2017)

Best Airline Worldwide, Best Economy Class and Airline with the Best Cabin Staff (Business Traveller Awards 2016)

Charitable Initiatives: The Emirates Airline Foundation – The foundation's aim is to help disadvantaged children realise their full potential by providing them with the basics, which most of us take for granted such as food, medicine, housing and education.

Notable Innovations: Emirates introduced new sustainable blankets for Economy Class passengers travelling on long-haul flights. Made from 100% recycled plastic bottles and using ecoTHREAD™ patented technology, these soft and warm blankets are environmentally friendly. Emirates launched the world's first interactive amenity kit for our Economy Class passengers. Utilising augmented reality technology in the kit bag design, customers can scan the kit bag using their mobile devices to experience exciting content during or after their flight.

Partners: Emirates have 22 codeshare partners in 26 countries.

Some of Emirates codeshare partners include:

- ✈ Alaska Airlines
- ✈ Malyaysia Airlines
- ✈ Korean Air
- ✈ Qantas
- ✈ Japan Airlines
- ✈ JetBlue Airways
- ✈ Thai Airways
- ✈ South African Airways

In 2013, Emirates entered a major partnership with Qantas. Together, Qantas and Emirates offer one of the most comprehensive international networks in the world.

Frequent Flyer Programme: The Emirates frequent flyer programme is called Skywards. As of 2016, the programme has 17 million members. The programme has four tiers: Blue, Silver, Gold and Platinum.

Aircraft Fleet: Emirates is the world's only airline to exclusively fly Airbus A380 and Boeing 777 aircraft. Emirates also operate one of the youngest fleet with an average age of just 61 months. The average age being 140 months.

As of March 2017, Emirates has 94 A380 aircraft with a further 48 on order. Just released in January 2018 is yet another deal for 38 more A380. As of November 2016, Emirates has 160 Boeing 777's, with a further 150 of the new 777x on order for 2020.

Classes of Travel: Emirates currently has three classes of travel: Economy, Business Class and First Class, with plans to introduce Premium Economy Class in the near future.

Route Network: Emirates route network spans 155 destinations, in 82 countries and across 6 continents.

CHEAT SHEET
IN DEPTH

FOR SERIOUS CANDIDATES

KEY FACTS

Slogan: The tagline was changed to "Hello Tomorrow" in 2012 from it's previous tagline "Fly Emirates, Keep Discovering". "Hello Tomorrow" aims to inspire consumers to greet tomorrow's unlimited potential. It is said that this slogan symbolises the pleasure in waking up to a brand new morning with Emirates.

IATA: EK

Headquarters: Garhoud, Dubai, United Arab Emirates

Hub: Dubai International Airport (DXB)

Commenced Operations: 25 October 1985. The first flight was the EK600 from Dubai International to Karachi

Parent Company: The Emirates Group

Brands: The Emirates Group owns the world's fourth largest airline and airport operations business 'dnata'. Other brands include Emirates SkyCargo, Arabian Adventures and Emirates Flight Catering.

Annual Passenger Numbers: 56,076 million (2016-2017 up 8.1% from 51,853 million (2015-2016)

Chairman & CEO: His Highness Sheikh Ahmed Bin Saeed Al Maktoum

President: Tim Clark

Employees: 64,768 (2016-2017) Including over 13,000 Cabin Crew. Emirates is a truly cosmopolitan airline, representing over 150 different nationalities

Call Sign: Emirates

The Emirates Logo: It is said that the red colour in the Emirates logo represents prosperity, self-confidence, passion and leadership. The white colour depicts nobility, elegance and purity.

RAPID EXPANSION

Emirates are incredibly driven in their business development and are constantly growing their brand. This is evident in the rapid expansion of the airline which has become one of the world's largest long haul airlines in just thirty years. According to the Emirates website, the airline adds an average of four new destinations every year and regularly increases flight frequencies. Emirates also continue to expand their fleet, averaging one new aircraft delivery each month. In 2016-17, Emirates added 35 new aircraft to its fleet.

In fact, Emirates made aviation history in 2003 when it struck the largest aircraft deal consisting of an order for 71 new aircraft at a list price of $19 billion USD.

AWARDS

World's Best Airline (Skytrax World Airline Awards 2016) This is the fourth time Emirates has won this top prize in the awards history.

World's Best Airline and Best Middle Eastern Airline (ULTRAS 2017)

Best Airline in the World (TripAdvisor Travellers Choice Awards 2017)

Best Airline Worldwide, Best Economy Class and Airline with the Best Cabin Staff (Business Traveller Awards 2016)

CHARITY INITIATIVES
The Emirates Airline Foundation

The foundation's aim is to help disadvantaged children realise their full potential by providing them with the basics, which most of us take for granted such as food, medicine, housing and education.

✈ **Housing**: The Emirates Airline Foundation aims to provide safety and security for destitute children by providing them with a roof over their heads.

✈ **Health**: The Emirates Airline Foundation aims to provide healthcare to children in need through projects like the Emirates Friendship Hospital Ship in Bangladesh and various projects in Africa, India, Sri Lanka and beyond.

✈ **Food**: The Emirates Airline Foundation aims to prevent children going hungry by providing them the means to basic nutritional requirements. The foundation reaches out to these children by paying for food supplies at various charities across our network.

✈ Education: The Emirates Airline Foundation aims to provide the **resources** needed to educate impoverished children so that they might develop the tools for a brighter tomorrow.

NOTABLE INNOVATIONS

Lounge and Shower: Emirates was the first airline to install a lounge and shower on its A380 aircraft.

Sustainable Blankets: Emirates introduced new sustainable blankets for Economy Class passengers travelling on long-haul flights. Made from 100% recycled plastic bottles and using ecoTHREAD™ patented technology, these soft and warm blankets are environmentally friendly, and reflect Emirates' commitment to product innovation and sustainability.

Interactive Amenity Kit: Emirates launched the world's first interactive amenity kit for our Economy Class passengers. Utilising augmented reality technology in the kit bag design, customers can scan the kit bag using their mobile devices to experience exciting content during or after their flight.

PARTNERS & ALLIANCES

While Emirates are not a member of an airline alliance, they do have 22 codeshare partners in 26 countries.

Some of Emirates codeshare partners include:

- ✈ Alaska Airlines
- ✈ Malyaysia Airlines
- ✈ Korean Air
- ✈ Qantas
- ✈ Japan Airlines
- ✈ JetBlue Airways
- ✈ Thai Airways
- ✈ South African Airways

In 2013, Emirates entered a major partnership with Qantas. Together, Qantas and Emirates offer one of the most comprehensive international networks in the world.

Together connecting the globe

FREQUENT FLYER CLUB

The Emirates frequent flyer programme is called Skywards. As of 2016, the programme has 17 million members.

The programme has four tiers:

- ✈ **Blue**: The basic level that all members join at.
- ✈ **Silver**: Awarded at 25,000 tier miles (25 qualifying flights)
- ✈ **Gold**: Awarded at 50,000 tier miles (50 qualifying flights)
- ✈ **Platinum**: Awarded at 150,000 tier miles (25 qualifying flights)

The number of miles earned depends on three factors, these are the cabin class, type of ticket and length of the flight.

AIRCRAFT FLEET

Emirates is the world's only airline to exclusively fly Airbus A380 and Boeing 777 aircraft. Emirates also operate one of the youngest fleet with an average age of just 61 months. The average age being 140 months.

As of March 2017, Emirates has 94 A380 aircraft with a further 48 on order. Just released in January 2018 is yet another deal for 38 more A380. As of November 2016, Emirates has 160 Boeing 777's, with a further 150 of the new 777x on order for 2020.

CLASSES OF TRAVEL

Emirates currently has three classes of travel: Economy, Business Class and First Class, with plans to introduce Premium Economy Class in the near future.

✈ **Economy**: On the Airbus A380, passengers benefit from 32-34 inches of seat pitch and an 18.5-inch wide seat. The Boeing 777 fleet has 32 inches of pitch and a 17-inch wide seat. Every seat is fitted with a personal in-flight entertainment system, called ice, which gives access to up to 2,500 channels of entertainment. Passengers are offered complimentary meals, snacks and a full bar service.

✈ **Business**: All seats in the Business Class cabin on board the A380 have direct aisle access and convert into a fully flat bed with a length of either 70 or 79 inches. Emirates is in the process of upgrading its 777 Business Class seats to a new design, inspired by the interior of a modern sports car, that can be converted into a 78-inch long fully flat bed.

✈ **First Class**: Passengers enjoy a private suite with sliding doors and a seat that converts into a 78-inch fully flat bed. The suite features a mini bar, vanity unit and large personal television screen. An onboard shower spa, allows first class passengers to freshen up prior to arrival at their destination.

ROUTE NETWORK

Emirates route network spans 155 destinations, in 82 countries and across 6 continents.

Emirates added its 12th destination in the United States with its new Fifth Freedom flight from Athens to Newark. The airline also serves Fort Lauderdale, Orlando, Chicago, Boston, San Francisco, Los Angeles, Seattle, Dallas, Houston, Washington and New York JFK.

 Check out the interactive route map on Emirates website.

NEW ROUTES

✈ Emirates added the following destinations in 2016: Cebu and Clark in the Philippines, Yinchuan and Zhengzhou in China, Yangon in Myanmar, Hanoi in Vietnam and Fort Lauderdale in the US.

✈ Emirates will launch a new service from Dubai to Zagreb, Croatia.

✈ From July 2017, a new service will operate from Dubai to Phnom Penh in Cambodia.

✈ Guinea rejoined the Emirates network in October 2016, with a four times weekly service to Conakry.

THAT'S A WRAP

That's a wrap for this session and you are now armed with some valuable information.

As you progress through this course, you will make good use of the information you have compiled.

For now, take a break, grab a cup of your favourite brew or whatever you fancy and come back when you are ready to start on Step 2 where you'll start to put together your application pack.

You are officially more informed than 90% of candidates who attend a cabin crew interview.

PART TWO
APPLY

There are two potential outcomes for this module, these are:

OUTCOME 1
APPLY FOR THE POSITION
If you have an airline in your sights and qualify for the role now, by the end of this module you are going to submit your application. Woo

OUTCOME 2
BE READY TO APPLY FOR THE POSITION
If, for any reason, you aren't ready to apply just yet, you will have the application ready for when that time does come. Whichever outcome is right for you at this time, you are going to come away from this module prepared with a killer application.

WHAT TO EXPECT

STEP 1 : Compile your résumé / CV Having a powerful resume will serve you well throughout the entire process. Within this step you'll create one that's perfect for you and your background

STEP 2 : Produce your photographs Photographs are an essential element for any airline application, and some airlines will have very strict requirements about their presentation.

STEP 3 : Complete the application form With the data gathered and application materials produced, now comes the exciting part. First we will examine typical questions and look at the most effective way to approach them, and then you will transfer your data into an actual application form that will be ready for submission.

STEP 4 : Submit the application form (Optional) By this step, you have a compelling and powerful application kit ready to submit to your chosen airline. Whoop whoop.

REFRESH
YOUR RESUME

INTRODUCTION

Within this section, we'll take a look at refreshing your resume, also referred to as a CV or curriculum vitae.

You may not need to submit your resume to Emirates, but it is useful for quick reference when filling out your application form and at the interview.

By the of this section, you'll have a strong resume, full of your accomplishments and skills that will be transferrable to your application.

KEY POINTS

Your résumé is a very powerful document because it represents the best you have to offer. To make this document even more powerful, we are going to take a look at the following three areas.

FORMAT

OUTLINE

OPTIMISE

CHOOSE YOUR RESUME FORMAT

Depending on your career path to date, you'll want to pick a format that will highlight your strengths and minimise any areas of perceived weakness. The three basic formats are:

Chronological
Functional
Combination

CHRONOLOGICAL

The chronological résumé highlights the dates, places of employment and job titles, having employment and education detailed first

IDEAL FOR
✈ Demonstrating career progression
✈ If you want to highlight your career within the airline industry

AVOID IF
✈ You have large gaps in employment or a chequered history
✈ Are going through a major career change

CHRONOLOGICAL OUTLINE
Here is a typical outline of a chronological format:

✈ Personal Information
✈ Career Summary
✈ Detailed Career History (In Reverse Chronological Order)
✈ Additional Skills & Achievements
✈ Education & Qualifications
✈ Interests & Hobbies
✈ References

The focus with this format is on your career history, so you will display the employer, date from and to, job title and a breakdown of your responsibilities starting from the most recent rst.

FUNCTIONAL

A functional résumé focuses on skills and achievements and uses functional headings, such as Sales, Customer Service and Teamwork, instead of the chronological employment data.

IDEAL FOR
✈ Downplaying an extreme career change
✈ Concealing large gaps in employment or a chequered employment history.
✈ To highlight a relevant skill set

AVOID IF
✈ You are a recent graduate or are lacking experience
✈ You lack relevant or transferable skills

FUNCTIONAL OUTLINE
Here is a typical outline of a funcational format:

✈ Personal Information
✈ Career Objective
✈ Career Summary
✈ Key Skills (Using functional headings such as sales, managerial, customer service, etc)
✈ Brief Education & Employment History
✈ Interests & Hobbies
✈ References

The format focuses more on key skills, so break those down into strong areas of interest to the airline, and elaborate on how these have been demonstrated. Rather than a detailed breakdown of your career and education, you will want to include just a brief overview.

COMBINATION

The combination résumé, is a combination of the chronological and functional formats.

IDEAL FOR
- Showcasing a relevant and developed skill set
- Making a career change
- Highlighting lots of relevant expertise

FUNCTIONAL OUTLINE
Here is a typical outline of a combination format:

- Personal Information
- Career Objective
- Career Summary
- Key Skills (Using functional headings such as sales, managerial, customer service, etc)
- Detailed Career History (In Chronological Order)
- Education & Qualifications
- Interests & Hobbies
- References

With this format, you will include both the key skills and a detailed career history. Key skills will come rst, with experience directly following.

MODIFIED COMBINATION
OUR CHOICE

For the purpose of the cabin crew position, I will take you through a slightly modified version of the combination format. This format has shown to be the most effective and rounded approach.

✈ Personal Information
✈ Objective Statement
✈ Key Skills
✈ Employment History
✈ Education & Qualifications
✈ Certifications
✈ Activities & Interests
✈ References

You may, of course, modify this if another format is better suited to you. Simply use the guidelines provided for that format.

LAYOUT
YOUR RESUME

PERSONAL INFORMATION

A rather obvious section, so I'll keep it brief. At the beginning of the résumé you are going to want to include your name, your home mailing address, your telephone number(s), and your e-mail address. If you have both temporary and permanent addresses, you may include them both.

OBJECTIVE STATEMENT

My objective.... To get the job duh!!!

Yes, that may well be true, but the objective statement requires more than "Hire me, I want the job"

Instead, the objective should define your career goals while also positioning you as the ideal candidate for the position. It is a brief and targeted statement that gives your résumé focus and a great opportunity to show how your skills relate to the airline and the position.

If you are going through a career change or are currently working freelance, the objective statement is especially useful as it demonstrates that you have given your career direction due consideration, while also explaining any inconsistencies that may exist.

COMMON MISTAKES TO AVOID

✈ **Making it all about you**

Example: "I have always loved to travel and am looking to join a prestigious airline that has lots of amazing destinations and where I can get cheap flights while meeting handsome wealthy men in first class....."

Okay, I am laying that one on thick, but you see my point. The objective is not about you or your needs, it is about what you bring to Emirates.

✈ **Being too vague**

Example: "Looking for a job as cabin crew with an airline where I can apply my extensive skills and experience."

Hmm, that's not very enticing is it?

Would you want to go through the time and expense of bringing this person to interview when they have some undefined skills and experience, and who seems to not care which airline they work for? No, and neither does Emirates.

✈ **Offering no value**

Example: "I have extensive skills in marketing and development..."

STOP!!! Back up a bit.

How is this relevant to a cabin crew position? That's right, it isn't. Next...

If you do come from a background that seems un-relatable, such as marketing and development, dig deeper. Instead of marketing, the ability to influence could be used, and, instead of development, the ability to manage a team.

Now those would be kick ass skills to include.

✈ zzzzzzz

Example: "My name is Jane Doe and I come from London, England. I have been working in nance, but I want to make a move to working as cabin crew. I have lots of skills, such as teamworking, customer service, and leadership. I also worked within......... and on, on on, and on......"

Just remember that this is a brief statement, not an essay. zzzzz sorry, dozed off there for a second. What were we talking about?

You get my point. Keep it short and snappy

HOW TO WRITE A SIZZLING OBJECTIVE

When writing your objective statement, there are four key points to keep in mind that will make it smoking hot.

✈ Be specific
✈ Focus on the benefits you offer
✈ Keep it short
✈ Make it relevant to the position

USE EMIRATES OWN KEYWORDS

Here is where the research you conducted in the research module will begin to pay off.

To make your objective even more powerful and specific, you are going to insert Emirates own person specification keywords right into your objective.

This is highly targeted and makes it easier to select qualities that the airline considers most valuable.

EXAMPLE OBJECTIVE STATEMENTS

✈ A hard working and reliable customer service advisor looking to apply 3+ years of customer facing experience and excellent interpersonal skills to a cabin crew role within Emirates.

✈ Seeking a cabin crew position with Emirates where my customer relationsexperience and warm interpersonal style can be effectively used to provide passengers with a first class and welcoming experience.

✈ Friendly and enthusiastic nurse who is looking to bring excellent interpersonal and communication skills, along with 4+ years of experience within the health care industry to the role of cabin crew within Emirates.

✈ A professional and reliable travel operator with 5+ years of experience within a customer facing and teamwork oriented role looking to bring an enthusiastic and personable nature to the role of cabin crew with Emirates.

TASK
WRITE YOUR OBJECTIVE

Using the examples above, and the key skills you developed in module one, have a go at writing out your own statement.

KEY SKILLS
Ah ha. My favourite bit.

The key skills section provides a fantastic opportunity for you to quickly express your suitability for the role and show what transferable skills you will bring. It will also bulk out your résumé with the keywords that will be picked up by OCR scanning technology (More on this later).

Key skills can be those gained through your work experience or hobbies, even though your studies and voluntary placements. This is why they are so valuable, especially if you have a short career history.

THREE SKILL CATEGORIES
Key skills t into the following three distinct categories:

✈ Transferable Skills
✈ Aptitude Skills
✈ Job Related Skills

TRANSFERRABLE SKILLS
Transferable skills are generally learned skills and include those that can be picked up from your hobbies and personal interests, volunteer work, employment or education and can be transferred across to any industry or position.

The transferable skills airlines are interested in include:

✈ Teamwork
✈ Foreign languages
✈ Time management
✈ Customer service
✈ Decision making
✈ Problem solving
✈ Leadership and management

APTITUDE SKILLS

Aptitude skills tend to overlap transferable skills, however, aptitude skills are those that are inherited as part of your character. Aptitude skills could include:

- Initiative
- Interpersonal skills
- Communication
- Adaptability
- Motivation
- Positive nature
- Tenacity
- Loyalty
- Friendly / sociable
- Logical

JOB RELATED SKILLS

Job related skills are those that are specific to an industry. The key here is to find relatable skills within that industry that could become transferable. For instance:

Hairdresser > transferrable skilll > Customer Service
Tour Guide > transferrable skill > Public Speaking
Nurse > transferrable skill > First Aid & Empathy
Travel Agent > transferrable skill > Currency Conversion
Call Centre Operator > transferrable skill > Handing Adversity
Interior Designerr > transferrable skill > Managing People
Self Employer > ransferrable skill > Self Starter
Technical Support > transferrable skill > Explain Complex Information Clearly

Whatever jobs you have held, look for a transferrable and relatable skill.. Highlight those as much as possible. Suddenly a seemingly irrelevant position can be seen as highly valuable.

EXAMPLE STATEMENTS

Once you have picked out 4 or 5 key skills, elaborate with short statements that provide insight to how you have applied these in the past. Here are some examples:

✈ **Extensive Interpersonal Skills**

Working as a personal trainer for the past 5 years has given me first hand experience working very closely with people from all backgrounds and of all ages.

✈ **Team Spirited and ability to use my own initiative**

Working as a waitress has given me an opportunity to develop my team working skills to a high standard, but it has also taught me to use my own initiative when working under pressure.

✈ **Problem Solver**

Working as a freelance designer has given me an opportunity to develop finely tuned problem solving skills. I am able to think fast on my feet and deal effectively with challenges that create a positive outcome.

✈ **Strong customer service skills**

As part of my job being a call centre handler, I have had the opportunity to develop a very rounded skill set that enables me to be empathetic to the customer, while also having the company interests in mind in order to ensure the best possible outcome for all concerned.

TASK
WRITE YOUR KEY SKILL STATEMENT

EMPLOYMENT HISTORY

Employment history should be displayed starting with your most recent position, working backwards and include the following elements:

✈ Name of employer
✈ Position held
✈ Period of employment
✈ Duties performed
✈ Achievements

DESCRIBING DUTIES

When describing your duties, there are three key points to bear n mind, these are:

✈ Use short action phrases
✈ Make it relatable
✈ Focus on results

ACTION PHRASES

Action phrases offer greater impact than compete sentences or generic job descriptions because being short and punchy allows for easy scanning. Here are some examples of such phrases:

✈ Supervised and trained a team of four junior-level stylists
✈ Manage and maintain a customer base of over 100 clients
✈ Maintain up to date records of customer accounts
✈ Ensure customer comfort and satisfaction
✈ Assist with enquiries and resolve complaints

RELATABLE

As we discussed earlier, the points of the job you want to extract and highlight, are those that are relatable to the position of cabin crew. Notice how breaking down the job of an interior designer below can appear totally different, depending on the words we use. Same job, different outcome and impression.

AVOID THIS...
✈ Develop & design interior concepts
✈ Consider materials and analyse costs
✈ Source products
✈ Survey building
✈ Blah, blah, blah...

DO THIS...
✈ Discuss client requirements
✈ Communicate & negotiate with suppliers
✈ Collaborate with a team of designers, architects and suppliers
✈ Supervise contractors to ensure the customer requirements are met

While the rst example has no relevant keywords, the second has plenty. Which resume do you think will fair better in the recruitment process?

RESULTS / ACCOMPLISHMENTS
If you have any notable achievements that can be quantied, be sure to mention those too. Here are some notable achievements worth mentioning:

✈ Increased customer loyalty or satisfaction
✈ Decreased customer complaints
✈ Developed an idea that saved time or money, increased productivity, etc.
✈ Awards won
✈ Promotions earned

Even those little compliments your supervisor or managers have made informally can add weight to your application and make for a good story to tell during your interview, so try to remember anything that may be relevant. Did you make a suggestion for improvements that your superior was particularly impressed by? Did you have an idea for a new service that was implemented? All these things matter.

MINIMISE FRAGMENTATION

If you have a fragmented work history, it will give the impression of a job hopper and this is something you will want to avoid. The good news is there are many things you can do to draw attention away and minimise the impact . So let's take a look at the options.

COMBINE JOBS

Where several similar consecutive jobs appear or were provided by the same agency, you can combine them into one chunk, for example:

2004–2006 // Front Desk Clerk
Aztec Hotel & Spa, Bloomfields Leisure, Trina's Hair & Beauty Salon

2001–2003 Customer service manager
CS Employment Agency

For summer jobs, you can avoid listing listing specific dates by using a range, for example:

Summer 20xx to Spring 20xx.

ELIMINATE POSITIONS

There are times when it is beneficial to simply drop a position from your résumé. Take a look at the chart below to determine if this could be right for you.

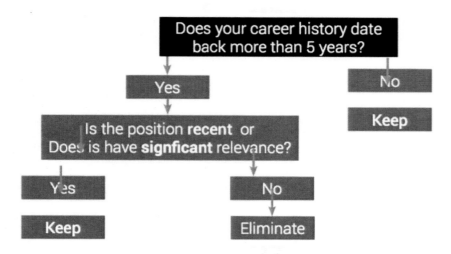

FILL THE GAPS

If you have gaps in your career progression, but were doing something notable during that time, paid or unpaid, you could insert this into the gap to eliminate any unnecessary questions or concern. For instance:

2004–2006 // Fitness Instructor
Bloom elds Leisure

2006-2007 // Traveled around Europe or Study Break
2007–2012 // Personal Trainer
Wilson Gym

When lling the gaps, observe caution about revealing too much about your personal circumstances. Revealing that you had taken maternity leave will highlight your parental status. Although this may seem harmless, it's not something to advertise when seeking employment.

Employment history is a broad term that can include relevant internships, summer or seasonal jobs, part time work, and voluntary placements. Even helping your pops with his self employment business or babysitting can be included if you are struggling to provide relevant experience. If you have major gaps to fll, take a look at what you were doing during those gaps and see if you can transfer and relate that across.

TASK
WRITE YOUR EMPLOYMENT HISTORY

EDUCATION & QUALIFICATIONS

This is a simple one. Starting with the most recent and working backwards, include the schools/colleges/universities you have attended. Within each entry, include the year of completion ("In progress" or "expected" are acceptable) and award(s) you achieved. Easy peasy.

If you are a mature candidate, and your qualifications go bad a way, you may leave off your high school and any dated qualifications that are irrelevant. These will only draw unnecessary attention to your age.

TASK
WRITE YOUR QUALIFICATIONS

CERTIFICATIONS

If you have attended any formal certification courses that are relevant, be sure to include these. Examples could be:

✈ First Aid
✈ Lifesaving
✈ Food Hygiene
✈ Teaching

TASK
WRITE YOUR CERTIFICATIONS

LANGUAGES

If you have more than one language ability, indicate whether you speak, read, and/or write the language, and include the level to which you are proficient, such as: native, fluent, proficient or basic conversational ability. If you only had High School training that you only remember two words from, you may want to leave that aside.

TASK
WRITE YOUR LANGUAGES

ACTIVITIES & INTERESTS

Recreational interests reveal a great deal about your personality and create depth to your character. Better yet, they also serve as excellent sources of additional skills and experiences which can be advantageous if you lack certain skills and/or experience. Most candidates miss this vital opportunity and ll the section with meaningless list statements or unprofessional revelations. Take a look at the following examples, and you'll understand the difference some ne tuning can make.

AVOID THIS ...
✈ Reading
✈ Watching television
✈ Going to the movies
✈ Socialising
✈ Traveling

AND DEFINITELY AVOID THIS ...
I enjoy spending time with my mates, hitting the town and going out on the razz.

DO THIS ...
I have been a keen netball player for as long as I can remember and am an active member of Anytown women's netball club where I have been captain of the team for 3 years. I have an active interest in nature, and regularly get involved with and manage conservation assignments. To relax, I attend yoga and meditation classes, which help to keep me focused and relieve any buildup of stress.

The statement on the right gives an immediate impression of someone who is balanced and committed. The interests highlight several admirable qualities such as team spirit and leadership, and it also details methods of stress management. A recruitment of cer would form a positive impression based on a statement such as this.

TASK
WRITE YOUR INTERESTS

REFERENCES

The inclusion of reference information is completely optional. When listing your references, be sure to include:

➤ Company
➤ Contact Name
➤ Job Title
➤ Date of Employment
➤ Telephone Number & Email
➤ Mailing Address

If you decide not to include details, simply state "References are available on request"

Always gain permission from those you state as your referee. You don't want a referee to refuse to provide a reference as this will reflect negatively.

TASK
GATHER REFERENCE INFORMATION

OPTIMISE
YOUR RESUME

Have you ever noticed how dull and boring resume's look?

Well, you'll be pleased to hear that won't be yours. Now that you've compiled your data, it's time to optimise it's appearance so that it gains attention and actually gets read. For this, we will look at the following elements:

COLOUR
LENGTH
STYLE

COLOUR

When used sparingly and consistently, colour can add life and interest to any dull resume. It can draw the eye to make the resume easier and more pleasant to read.

So, what exactly is consistent and sparingly?

LENGTH

For a cabin crew position, one or two pages is ideal. However, don't be constrained by this advice if doing so will mean that you have to squeeze your data in with a teeny tiny 8 point font.

If you do find your résumé going beyond this quota, just be sure that it isn't being filled with unnecessary, unfocused or excessive detail.

If your career history dates back 10 or more years, you may choose to eliminate some of the older positions.

Note: Stick to single sided prints for a cleaner look

STYLE

✈ Paper
A quality, medium weight paper will give your resume an important feel and will show you have given it's presentation a conscious effort.

✈ Margins
White space on the page will keep your resume from looking cramped and overwhelming. Keep a margin of at least 0.75"

PERSONAL LOGO

If you want to add a creative edge, a personal logo is a great way to add a bit of sparkle that looks professional and stands out, but without additional clutter.

The logo need not be fancy or use special software, the autographed designs below were created with a font called Biloxi Script that can be downloaded for free from DaFont. The Jane Doe design simply has a line added to the J. Nothing fancy, but can make a difference.

Some free font ideas that make great personal logos are:

✦ Biloxi Script

✦ **Bromello**

✦ Angelina

✦ Angelnova

✦ Always forever

OCR TECHNOLOGY

To facilitate more efficient processing of résumés, and applications, airlines use a computerised tracking system. This system uses OCR (Optical Character Recognition) technology.

This technology scans for specific keywords that indicate a particular set of skills, qualifications and experience.

Following the scan, a score will be awarded based on the number of 'hits'. From this score, the system will either generate a letter of invitation, or a letter of rejection.

To ensure a high score, and an invitation letter, it is essential that you learn and inject as many keywords as possible throughout your resume. Following are some sample power statements and power verbs to give you an idea what you can include.

✈ Good communication and interpersonal skills
✈ A confident and friendly personality
✈ Extensive customer service experience
✈ Confidence in dealing with a range of people
✈ The ability to work effectively in a team
✈ Ability to handle difficult customers firmly and politely
✈ Ability to stay calm, composed and focused under pressure
✈ The ability to be tactful and diplomatic, but also assertive

Action verbs express action. They are positive, powerful and directive, and should be used abundantly throughout your résumé.Here are just a few examples:

✈ Arranged   ✈ Assisted
✈ Communicated   ✈ Conveyed
✈ Directed   ✈ Explained
✈ Expressed   ✈ Generated
✈ Guided   ✈ Handled
✈ Improved   ✈ Incorporated
✈ Interacted   ✈ Listened
✈ Participated   ✈ Persuaded
✈ Provided   ✈ Resolved
✈ Suggested   ✈ Trained

CASE STUDY: ELLETTE MORGAN

Background

Ellette had always wanted to be cabin crew, but her early attempts ended in failure.

Confused about what jobs to take while she waited for her dream job, Ellette fell into the job hopping cycle.

As time went on, the job hopping cycle began to reflect badly on Ellette's CV and Ellette just ended up adding more interview failures to her list.

Losing all hope Ellette, eventually gave up on her dream.

After being a job hopper for several years, Ellette finally made her mark by becoming a freelancer, first as a nail technician and then as a graphic and web designer. Although happy in her profession, the dream career that escaped her continued to plague her mind and, finally, she decided to give it another shot.

After attending 3 interviews, each ending in further failure, Ellette came to me for assistance.

Concerns

Although Ellette had several years of face to face experience in dealing with customers and suppliers, the concerns that arose during interviews were focused on Ellette's early job hopping experience and her long history of being self employed.

The Airlines' Point of View

From the point of view of the airline, someone who has been in self employment for extended periods have adapted to not having a boss to report back to.

The concern is that such an applicant will struggle to reintegrate into mainstream employment. Ellette's history of job hopping only served to highlight those concerns further.
Solutions

Two major overhauls were included as part of Ellette's CV makeover.

First, the focus of the CV is now centred on the skills she has developed, and those that are transferrable within her role.

Next we removed Ellette's job history beyond the most recent two positions. Although this only leaves the CV with freelance positions, this has also been downplayed by using her business name in place of the employers name.

The removal of the fragmented history and references to self employment diffuses any initial concerns and objections that may arise before the interview takes place. If the recruiters are interested in Ellette's history beyond those provided, Ellette is able to explain those more effectively in a face to face meeting where objections can be raised and diffused.

Where a longer career history is required, we would look into combining consecutive jobs as outlined in the resume guidelines section of this module.

Ellette Morgan

"I am looking to provide a memorable passenger experience as a member of the Virgin Atlantic cabin crew team"

Key Skills

Exceptional People Skills
Over the years, I have worked hard to develop my interpersonal and people skills so that I am able to deliver a level of service that is far and beyond what clients expect. I pride myself on my ability to engage with others on a professional and personal level.

Self Starter and Detail Oriented
Over the years, I have had to develop a strong sense of initiative and drive in order to remain at the forefront of business. I am a self starter who is able to work unsupervised without external motivation, but am also able to work as part of a unified team in order to meet deadlines and exceed client expectations.

Ability to work under pressure
Working to deadlines and making informed decisions is an ongoing part of my everyday life. Over the years, I have learnt to work under such pressure, while maintaining a high standard of service. Often, my best work is produced when there is an element of pressure involved.

Strong work ethic
My work ethic is one of my greatest assets. I take great pride in providing a great service and exceeding expectations. I take great pride in going that extra mile.

Career History

Graphic and Web Designer   July 05 - Present

- » Liasing with clients during the initial briefing and offering ongoing support
- » Negotiating and liasing with a team of contractors and suppliers
- » Project management and supervision of work on site
- » Working out costs and preparing estimates
- » Ensuring customer satisfaction and demonstrating empathy towards clients
- » Resolving any problems or faults during the work process
- » Business management activities, including bookkeeping and tax returns, marketing and public relations.

Nail technician   December 01 - July 05

- » Consult and advise clients
- » Make clients feel comfortable and welcome.
- » Ensure client satisfaction
- » Initiate hygiene procedures and safe usage and storage of chemicals
- » Manage and maintain a customer base of over 100 clients
- » Provide a friendly and professional service
- » Maintain up to date records and accounts

Ellette Morgan

Continued from page 1

Education Summary

National Design Academy (2015)
[Nottingham University]
Foundation Degree in Interior Design [Distinction]

National Design Academy (2013)
[Nottingham University]
AIM Level 3 Diploma in Interior Design

Filton College (1997)
BTEC First Diploma in Performing Arts

Patchway High School (1996)
7 GCSE's

Certifications

First Aid (2010)
[St John's Ambulance]

Advanced First Aid (2011)
[St John's Ambulance]

Heathy & Safety (2012)
[City of Bristol College]

Personal Interests

I like to keep myself fit and healthy, and so I maintain a very active lifestyle which includes regular trips to the gym and yoga classes. I also have an interest in the fitness and bodybuilding competition industry, and have recently began competing myself. I first took to the stage last year at the Miami Pro show where I placed 6th. Not only is this one of the greatest challenges of my life, it also deomonstates my greatest strengths which is my determination and dedication.

I love to run, and often run 5 miles to keep me focused and relieves any build-up of stress. Not long ago before the fitness show, I was involved in the Bristol 10k where I raised over £1000 for the 'Make-a-Wish Foundation'. This marathon was defintely a challenge.

I also have a love for the aviation industry, so I often take weekends away to the Renaissance hotel in Heathrow, where I book a room overlooking the runway. This is where I get my inspiration to write and design, and also set goals for the future. More recently, I have also begun taking flying lessons. One day I would love to achieve my Private Pilots Licence (PPL).

"The flight is part of the travel experience and I would like to be involved in making it just as memorable as the destination"

NAIL THE
APPLICATION FORM

Okay, so you have your resume, now it's time to begin the all important step of filling in the application form.

With your resume completed, the application form will be a breeze as you'll simply need to transfer the data across. If you haven't completed the resume action steps, please go back and do those before progressing onto this section as I'll not repeat anything that has already been covered.

Unlike a resume, which can be manipulated to a certain degree, an application form is far more rigid. With its standardised format, comparisons between candidates and against the hiring criteria can be made momentarily, leaving no room for error.

In the following pages, I'll take you through the elements that are unique to the application form with some guidance on how to complete those parts effectively,.

APPLICATION TIPS

The perfect application

As well as the role requirements, there's a little more that great cabin crew members offer.

You should be determined to always perform well. And no doubt you'll be able to manage a pretty demanding work schedule.

Also, you'll be culturally aware and reflect who we are – professional, empathetic, progressive, visionary and cosmopolitan. These are the characteristics we look for when you meet us at an assessment day, so come prepared to demonstrate these qualities individually and in the group exercises we prepare for you.

(Source: Emirates Careers Website)

Within this section, I'll fill you in on the little nuances that are unique to the application form, these are:

✈ Dealing with dismissals
✈ Additional information
✈ Supplementary questions

DEALING WITH DISMISSALS

If you have a termination on your record, the airline will not care if the termination was unjust, unfair or has a good explanation, a termination is a big red flag and your application will likely be rejected. Because of this, you'll want to do all you can to downplay this.

There are several options you have for this, these are:

✈ Eliminate the position
✈ Adjust the reason
✈ Explain and downplay

How you deal with this is completely your choice. I will advise you on each of these outcomes,. but you will need to make the final judgement call as to how to proceed.

Eliminate the position

In the first instance, you may choose to omit the information and the position from your application. Omitting details is not the same as telling an outright lie or making a false statement. You will simply be striking the position from the record.

Eliminating a position will only work if you can answer yes to one or more of the following questions:

✈ You have sufficient work experience beyond this position
✈ The position you were terminated from was a long time ago
✈ The position was temporary or very short term

The only thing I will say with regard to this particular strategy is, airlines operate in a very security conscious industry. You only want to take this route if necessary. Don't use it for any recent, long term or important roles as it is likely you will be found out eventually.

Adjust the reason

A better option for a lot of people is to adjust the reason for dismissal. There are two options for this:

If you have just been red from your most recent employment, the airline will not know unless you tell them. So you could mark your employment to present and leave it at that. If asked if they can call your employer for a reference, it would not raise any eyebrows if you respectfully decline due to your ongoing employment.

The second option is to take proactive measures to have the termination designation changed. If the termination occurred some time ago, it is more likely that the employer will be open to changing the designation if you accept responsibility and demonstrate a sincere regret for the situation.

Simply advise them that the termination is damaging your chances of gaining employment and you would like the designation changed to something neutral, such as laid off or resigned.
Explain and downplay

If you would feel uncomfortable or unethical to omit such a detail and would prefer to take accountability for what happened, be sure to downplay the termination on your application form by simply stating 'will explain at interview'.

You will have some damage control to contend with, so remember to accept the mistake, don't blame others and don't make any excuses.

Stick to the facts, point out what went wrong and what you have learned from the experience.

Whichever route you take, there is a risk. Either you will not be hired by admitting to the termination or you may not be hired because you did not disclose it and were caught out. The decision has to be yours.

ADDITIONAL INFORMATION

At the end of most application forms, you will be presented with some form of additional information box. This box may be ambiguous and simply state 'Additional Information', or it could be more specific, such as: Please state your reason for applying and why you feel you are suited to the position of cabin crew?

However this box is worded, this is an opportunity to sell yourself and should never ever be left blank. Use it to provide a power statement that summarises your experience, highlights your key skills, and shares your motives all within a few short paragraphs.

I would suggest a 3 part format for answering such spaces:

✈ Highlight what you have to offer
✈ Explain why you are suitable
✈ Summarise your strengths

Don't let modesty prevent you from mentioning your strengths, this is the opportunity to shine, however, keep this section to 2-3 short and punchy paragraphs and no more. You want to leave some cards on the table.

Remember to insert those power key words.

Consider the following example:

"As you will note, my application form highlights my extensive eight years experience within the retail industry. Within which, I have built a solid foundation of customer relations and team working experience, both of which have enabled me to sharpen my communication and interpersonal skills.

With the skills I have developed and the experiences I have dealt with as a customer relations manager, combined with my passion for the airline industry, my motivation to succeed and strong work ethic, I am con dent that I will make a positive contribution to Fly High Airlines and excel as a member of the Fly High cabin crew team.

I would welcome the opportunity to meet with you to discuss this position and my background in more detail, and to explore ways I could contribute to the ongoing success of Fly High Airlines.

Thank you for your time and consideration. I look forward to hearing from you."

SUPPLEMENTARY QUESTIONS

In addition to the request for further information, the application may pose questions related to your motives for applying. These could include why you want to work for the airline, why you want to be cabin crew, or even why you believe you are the best person for the position.

Because the questions vary so much in nature, and because I have provided detailed guidelines to formulating answers in module 4, I won't go into detail here. If you do find any questions beyond the scope of this section, please visit the section related to questions and answers for more suggestions.

POWER UP YOUR APPLICATION

If during this process you have noticed a lack of skills to put forward, all is not lost. There are several other steps you can take to power up your application and give it some pizzazz. Take a look at the following options:

✈ **Boost your experience**

Experience within a customer-facing role is vital, so if this aspect of your application is shallow or weak, you should certainly consider taking on some additional short-term volunteer or evening work to compensate and strengthen your candidacy. Taking on additional work will show initiative and demonstrate a willingness to work and improve.

✈ **Take on volunteer work**

Volunteering is beneficial to your application in so many ways. Firstly, it will demonstrate a compassionate and caring side to your personality. Secondly, it will enable you to gain experience and flesh out your skill-set. And third, it will show that you are not motivated by monetary gain. As a side bene t, you will also gain additional referees who can vouch for you.

✈ **Learn new skills**

Taking the time to learn new skills will demonstrate your continued dedication to self-improvement and your effort in readying yourself for the position. So consider signing up for mini courses that will be relevant to the position, such as first aid, languages, assertiveness, communication, and leadership. Neither will take much time or money, but the value added to your resume will be substantial.

✈ **Engage in extra-curricular activities**

Extra-curricular activities can be a hidden gem when it comes to learning new skills and are often under-utilised. If you participate in team sports, it can demonstrate your ability to be a team player. If you coach little league, it will demonstrate your ability to be a leader and if you regularly participate in aerobic activities, it will show that you take pride in your health and fitness. So go out there and have some fun while boosting your candidacy all at the same time.

✈ **Mind the gap**

If you are between work when you apply, this can create a damaging gap that will need some explaining or give the wrong impression about your motives. Rather than do nothing during this period of downtime, be proactive by taking on some volunteer work, learning a new skill or sign up for a short course at your local college..

ACE THE
VIDEO INTERVIEW

On demand video interviews allow Emirates to assess potential candidates for cabin crew roles without going through the time and expense of inviting them to an on-site interview.

Unfortunately, it is also a fast and efficient way to eliminate large numbers of candidates from the thousands of applications they receive and is the exact reason why you need to be fully prepared before you attempt it for yourself.

At this stage of the process, Emirates aren't looking to screen for the right candidates, that comes later. Right now, their primary goal is to weed out the unsuitable candidates.

A peak behind the scenes

The best way to understand how the video interviewing works is to look at the company that produce the technology., which is HireVue.

https://www.hirevue.com/products/video-interviewing/ondemand

Task

Before we go any further, it will help you to know how these technologies work. Rather than me reiterating what these companies have already written, please take 5 minutes to peruse their websites and get a general overview. Once you have done that, return to this section and I'll guide you through the important aspects.

What you need to know

These video intelligence systems have very smart learning algorithms installed that have been developed in conjunction with psychologists and behaviour specialists. These algorithms analyse set data points and then predicts the future behaviour of each candidate based on those found.

In fact, the software analyses 15,000 Predictive Attributes. These attributes include:

✈ Eye movements
✈ Facial expressions
✈ Body movements
✈ Nuances of the voice
✈ Level of engagement
✈ The words you use
✈ The complexity of your words
✈ Motivation
✈ Level of distress
✈ Personality style

Based on all these elements combined, the technology will present a detailed report for the airline to analyse. It can even suggest who is suitable to be invited for further assessment and recommend follow-up questions.

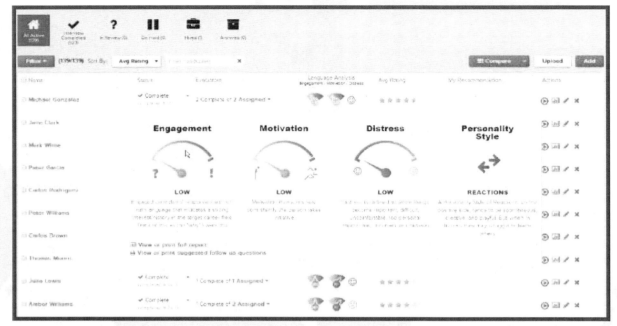

Photo Credit: Hirevue

The recommendations

As you can now appreciate, these video interviews are not to be approached haphazardly and preparation is the key to success.

How the scoring system works

The scoring system is based on pre-defined requirements chosen by the hiring manager. These requirements are made up of qualities and behaviours that the airline deem to be essential for the role of cabin crew.

These will be based on corporate culture and the person specification as detailed in the first module.

✈ Caring and friendly nature
✈ A positive attitude
✈ Professional
✈ Confidence
✈ Clear communication skills

The answers you give and the way you present yourself will all be sized up against these attributes.

How it works

✈ You'll complete the interview as part of the overall application

✈ Clicking on the link will take you to the online platform where you will see important information about your interview, including the number of questions and duration

✈ The platform will check that your recording equipment is working correctly

✈ You'll see a short introduction video that explains the interview process

✈ You have to do a practice question before starting the interview, which you can replay to yourself (no-one else will see this)

✈ Questions are given in written format. You'll have 30 seconds to get ready and one minute to respond.

✈ The interview will typically take 10 minutes to complete including your prepraation time between each answer.

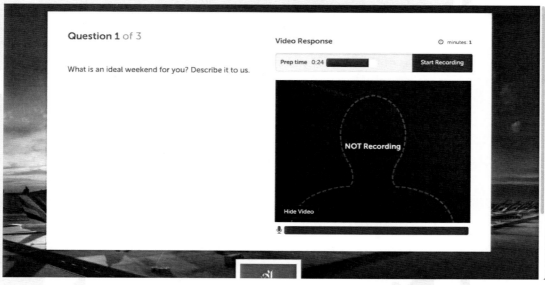

Get your tech set up

Before you attempt to perform the video interview, it is essential that you are fully prepared for it so that you can make the very best impression. Here are some guidelines that will help your interview go smoothly.

✈ Maintain a full battery or connect to a power supply

It's obvious, but easily missed. There is nothing more stress inducing than getting a battery low message half way through the most important interview of your life.

✈ Take note of your surroundings

Going through your video interview with a cluttered background is distracting and will not create a positive impression. Find a wall or nice view you can use for your backdrop but be conscious of a distracting background, such as a window or open door where there may be activity.

✈ Tend to lighting

Once you have a great location, be sure there is adequate lighting that is also flattering. Harsh shadows that create darkness around your eyes is never a good look. Position yourself so your light source comes from behind the webcam to shine on your face.

✈ Choose the right angle

Placing your computer or tablet at the wrong angle can create unflattering distortions in your features. The height of the webcam should be roughly eye level. Point the webcam down rather than pointing up under your chin for the best visual angle. Be sure it's not too close to your face, or too far away:

✈ Get connected to a strong internet signal

The last thing you want to happen is a failed connection, so get hooked up to a secure and stable line.

✈ Beware of background noise

Any background noise from televisions, fans, people walking by on the street, etc. should be kept to a minimum. If using a microphone, move the microphone closer to your voice and away from your computer where it may pick up the sound of your computer fan.

Typical Webcam Set-up
Not Optimal

Candidate looking down

Webcam too low

No flattering
lighting

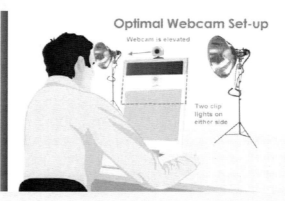

Optimal Webcam Set-up

Webcam is elevated

Two clip
lights on
either side

Get yourself prepared

The most important of all is how you present yourself, so approach the interview the right way with these simple tips for success.

✈ **Dress for an interview**

Dress professionally as you would for an in-person interview. Avoid patterns if possible and opt for solid colours that contrast against your background as this will transfer better on camera.

✈ **Get yourself fired up beforehand**

An advantage to having your interview in the comfort of your own home is that you are able to get yourself psyched up before you get on camera. This is a trick I learnt from my posing instructor when I competed in a fitness competition. Put your favourite music on and dance around the house. Doing this will loosen up your body and help to release any nervous energy. Trust me, it works.

✈ **Jot down some key points**

Write a short list of bullet points for some of the most important aspects you want to remember and pin it up near your monitor for quick reference.

✈ **Know your resume**

Be prepared to answer any question by knowing your resume thoroughly. Choose a time that suits you. The benefits of having an on-demand interview is that you can choose a time and day that you feel at your best.

Choose a time when you:

✈ Are well rested
✈ Are looking and feeling good
✈ Have the time and space to do the interview without being interrupted
✈ Have mentally prepared yourself
✈ Have rehearsed

Be aware of your body language

Even though the video will only be recording your head and shoulders, your body language is still important. In particular, you will want to be aware of the following aspects:

✈ **Consider your facial expressions**
The technology is analysing your features and behaviour, so consider the impact of your faction expressions. Aim to appear confident, happy, approachable and use a warm smile where appropriate

✈ **Avoid fidgeting**
Keep your hands away from your face and out of sight of the camera as much as possible.

Prepare for potential questions

The questions you may be asked will vary from airline to airline and may be changed from time to time, so there is no way to predict which questions you will be asked. However, there are some questions that are almost guaranteed to be asked, these are:

✈ Can you tell me about yourself and your work history?
✈ Why do you want to work for us?
✈ What interests you about this job?
✈ What skills can you bring to the position?
✈ Why do you want to become cabin crew?
✈ What do you value most in a friendship and why?

In addition, you will most likely be asked some behavioural style questions related to customer service and teamwork experience, for example:

✈ Tell me about a time when you have gone out of your way for a customer
✈ Tell me about a time when you have worked well as part of a team
✈ Tell me about a time when you handled a customer complaint
✈ Tell me about a time when you handled adversity

You can find more detailed guidelines for answering questions within the final interview module of this course.

Rehearse

Rehearsing before you do the interview for real is the best way to get confident in front of the camera and be sure that you will come across positively.

Give it a try beforehand. Grab your laptop, tablet or mobile phone and go through a few dry runs. Try answering the questions above in real time and see how you come across.

When going over your rehearsal recording, take note of the following:

✈ How do your answers sound?
✈ How many times did you say 'um' or 'er'?
✈ Were there long, uncomfortable pauses?
✈ Were you fiddling with anything?
✈ What were your facial expression like?

PRODUCE
PERFECT PHOTOS

The requisition of photographs is so much more than a simple vanity requirement, and I cannot emphasise their importance enough.

Not only will they serve as a visual reminder for the recruiters to refer back to throughout the assessment process, but they are also used to make hiring decisions long after the interview is over.

Emirates in particular are very strict when it comes to photo standards, and so you should follow their guidelines exactly. We will cover those guidelines in more detail.

As part of the application process, you'll be required to submit the following photographs:

✈ Formal full length photo
✈ Casual full length photo
✈ Casual half-length photo
✈ Formal passport size photo

DIY OR GO PRO

Where formal photos are requested, Emirates will only accept unedited and professional studio photos. This guideline is very strict and must be followed exactly.

SETTING THE SCENE

For your formal shots, Emirates are very specific with the backdrop, so be sure to follow those exactly. Get in the studio and have your photos taken on a white backdrop without any props. No exception.

For your informal shots, be sure they are tasteful pictures where you are fully clothed. Having photos of you taken with a scenic backdrop is a good option that always goes down well. Be sure that you are smiling in whatever photo you select.

WARM YOUR SMILE

A warm and sincere smile will complete the look, but creating a beautiful smile on demand is a learned skill which needs to be practiced.

The fake smile, aptly named the 'Pan-Am Smile' because of the flight attendants of Pan-American Airlines, is simply a courtesy smile that will not translate well in your photos. A 'Duchenne Smile', on the other hand, will provide the most beautiful and sincere looking smile, and this is the smile we are looking to achieve.

Here are some tips that will assist you in generating your photo perfect smile.

Produce a natural smile

The most beautiful smiles are the ones that are natural. If you are using a professional photographer, they will be skilled at drawing out your natural smile, but if you are using an unskilled family member, you will need to channel some of your inner happiness.

This can be achieved by thinking of a genuine reason to smile, such as recalling a happy memory, looking at a silly picture, or remembering a good joke.

Fake it till you make it

When it is simply impossible to summons a genuine smile, you will need to fake it. Here's some guidelines that will help.

✈ Time it right:

The secret to producing a relaxed and natural smile is to time it so that you don't have to hold it for too long. Try looking away from the camera, then just before the photograph is taken, face the camera and smile.

✈ Use your eyes:

Smiling eyes are required to complete the look. To achieve this effect, imagine the camera is someone you really fancy. Raise your eyebrows and cheekbones a little, and slightly squint the corners of your eyes. Notice the amazing transformation this creates.

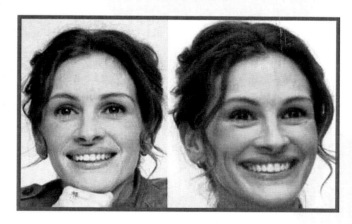

See the difference?

The image on the left is a Pan-Am smile. The right, a beautiful Duchenne Smile

Case Study: My faux pas

After my final interview with Emirates, I received a telephone call from the recruiter who interviewed me advising that the photographs I had submitted weren't up to their standard and would likely be rejected by their Dubai HR team. She gave me full instructions for the photograph requirements and asked that I resubmit them before my application was sent off for final processing and a hiring decision made.

I submitted a new set of photographs, but still tried to get around their specifications, and I was again told they would be rejected due to being digitally processed. At that time in my life, I was fearful of the camera and appearing un-photogenic so I done another set and attempted to process them so the recruiter wouldn't know they were digital. It didn't work, she called me once again to request a correction.

Finally I spent money to have my photos taken in a studio and they were accepted.

This story demonstrates just how important photos can be, but also how a recruiter who believes in you can go out of their way to help you succeed, even after you fluff up a few times.

Take away point, please follow their standards exactly. No cutting corners.

My photos are presented on the following pages for your learning purposes.

Female photos:

- Business attire with closed fitted jacket, knee length skirt, skin colour stockings and closed toe heels

- Smart casual wear – we suggest jeans and a plain coloured t-shirt with closed toe high heels

- No accessories

- Hair should be neatly tied

- Full make up

- Full length photo (from the top of your head to your shoes)

- Stand up straight with arms straight down by your side and both legs together

- Face the camera straight on and ensure the photo is sharp and in focus

- Find good lighting to avoid shadows

- Plain background for your formal photo

- And above all else please remember to smile

Male photos:

- Business attire with closed jacket, shirt and tie

- Smart casual wear – we suggest jeans and a plain coloured t-shirt with closed shoes

- No accessories

- Short hair neatly presented with minimal styling product

- Clean shaven

- Full length photo (from the top of your head to your shoes)

- Stand up straight with arms straight down by your side and both legs together

- Face the camera straight on and ensure the photo is sharp and in focus

- Find good lighting to avoid shadows

- Plain background for your formal photo

- And above all else please remember to smile

Photo Credit: Emirates Careers

PART THREE
PREPARE

PREPARE
FOR THE BIG DAY

The Run Up to the Big Day

✈ Rehearse
On the final run up to the event, set aside some time to go through a final rehearsal of your presentation. Practice answering questions and going over talking points with a friend or relative and use this opportunity to iron out any wrinkles.

✈ Perform a dry run
If possible, take the opportunity to visit the venue in advance. This dry run will familiarise you with the route, parking and travel time and allow you to avoid becoming lost or late on the day. If you can do the route at the same time of day, you'll benefit from the added simulation of traffic and road conditions. If you are unable to make an advance visit the venue, use the internet to map out a detailed route map that also provides distance and time estimations.

✈ Inspect your outfit

A few days before the event, take out the outfit you plan to wear and make sure it is clean, pressed, and has no buttons missing. Have it dry cleaned and repaired if necessary.

✈ Get a hair cut

Consider having your hair cut a week out from the day. This will allow the cut to soften slightly for a more natural look, while still retaining some of the freshness of the cut.

✈ Calm your nerves

If you feel your anxiety levels begin to escalate, put aside time to practice the strategies outlined in the previous section

The Evening Before

✈ Review your résumé

As you complete a final review of your résumé, notice and take pride in your listed achievements. Take the time to remind yourself of why you want the job and what you have to offer.

✈ Check travel arrangements

If travelling by car, make sure the tank has plenty of petrol and that you have change available for parking meters. If using public transport, check timetables.

✈ Prepare your outfit

Take out the outfit you plan to wear and go through a final inspection to make sure it is clean and pressed. Inspect your hosiery for runs or holes. Clean and polish your shoes. Prepare your accessories and gather your portfolio pieces. Then, lay the pieces out ready for the morning.

✈ Organise your portfolio
To avoid a morning rush, prepare your portfolio in advance.

✈ Get an early night
To ensure you are fresh and alert, you'll need a good night's sleep. So, aim to retire no later than 11 pm. A warm aromatherapy bath before bed will help you relax and unwind.

✈ Set your alarm (or two)
Before winding down for the night, ensure your alarm is set to the appropriate time. For caution, you may set two alarms or enlist a relative to give you a friendly wake up call.

On the Day

✈ Drink a glass of water
As soon as you rise, rehydrate and wake up your system with a large glass of water.

✈ Stretch
Incorporating a full body stretch into your morning routine will increase blood flow and wake up your tired muscles.

✈ Psyche yourself up
Jump start your motivation by chanting your incantations, acknowledging your goals and visualising your success.

✈ Listen to music
Listening to your favourite upbeat music is a great way to put you in a good mood. It will lighten the atmosphere and increase your energy level.

✈ Eat a good breakfast
Oatmeal is light, natural and slow releasing so it will provide ample energy for the day. Perhaps combine it with a protein shake and piece of fruit for a power breakfast.

✈ Leave with plenty of time to spare
Arriving late to an interview means you immediately start the interview from behind the rest of the candidates. You also risk arriving in a panic. You should, therefore, aim to arrive at least 15 minutes early and allow extra travelling time to account for any unforeseen delays.

It is better to be an hour early than it is to be just a minute late. You can always grab a coffee and go through your notes.

On Arrival

✈ Freshen up
If you have time, and it's convenient to do so, take a moment when you arrive to freshen up. Inspect your outfit, wash your hands, touch up your makeup, pop in a breath mint and spritz some deodorant. Be sure to discard any gum or breath mints before you enter the announce your arrival.

✈ Turn off your cell phone
To avoid potential interruptions, turn off your cell phone or put it on silent mode as soon as you arrive.

Portfolio Essentials

✈ Copies of your résumé
✈ Interview invitation
✈ A copy of your application form
✈ Passport
✈ Certificates
✈ Reference details
✈ Photographs

You should take one full length with one or two passport sized.

✈ A notepad
A notepad is tidier than lots of pieces of paper.

✈ 2 pens
With two pens, you will have a backup if the first runs out of ink or becomes lost. Alternatively, you can lend one to another candidate.

✈ A pencil and eraser
These two items are a must as they will make any mistakes easy to rectify.

CREATE
A MEMORABLE IMPRESSION

INVENT YOUR INTRODUCTION

First impressions are absolutely critical for interview success. The impression you provide within the first few minutes will be the one that sticks and, anything following, will become merely a confirmation of that first impression. So, to assist you in getting off to the very best start, I have devised some tips that will make you appear confident, friendly, relaxed and professional.

Upon Arrival

"Hello. My name is Jane Doe and I'm here for an interview with Caitlyn Rogers"
Once signed in, thank the receptionist and take a seat in the waiting area.

Meeting the candidates

If you are attending an open day or group selection process where other candidates will be present, you will have many introductions to contend with. These introductions are just as important as any other and must not be underestimated.

Candidate introductions should be handled in much the same way as any other, however, you may keep these slightly less formal if you wish. As you approach the candidate(s), smile and make eye contact, then say hello and introduce yourself. In a one to one introduction, offer a handshake if you so desire. In a group introduction, a handshake is unnecessary. If the candidate(s) responds positively to your approach, you may engage in further small talk.

Meeting the recruiter(s)

When you meet each recruiter for the first time, be sure to stand up straight, make eye contact and smile. Then, allow the recruiter to initiate the introduction and the handshake.

✈ If they greet you by name, your response should be: "Hello Ms. Rogers. It's a pleasure to meet you".

✈ If an introduction is needed, simply say: "I'm Jane Doe. It's a pleasure to meet you" or "Hello Ms. Rogers. Pleased to meet you. I'm Jane Doe"

At this stage, pleasantries may be initiated by the recruiter as a way to break the ice. Just follow their lead and go with the flow.

PLAN AN EXIT STRATEGY

When the interview approaches its conclusion, regardless of what has happened and how we feel, it is important to depart gracefully for that final lasting impression.

✈ Step 1: Gather your belongings
Before rising, gather your belongings and ensure a firm grip. If possible, leave your right hand free for the inevitable final handshake.

✈ Step 2: Straighten your clothing
As you rise from your seat, be sure to straighten up any disjointed attire such as your tie, jacket or skirt.

✈ Step 3: Exchange pleasantries
Once standing, smile and say "Thank you for taking the time to meet with me today". Then, if expected, exchange handshakes and make your way to the door.

✈ Step 4: Make your exit
Stop at the door, turn, smile and say a final "thank you". Then proceed with your exit and be sure to close the door behind you.

THE POSITIVE
FIRST IMPRESSION

Now that you've researched the airline and compiled a kick-ass portfolio, it's time to get prepared for the interview. So, in this step three, we'll explore how to dress to impress.

First, the myths

Before we continue on I feel it is important to address some of the myths that are circulating with regards to appearance.

These myths usually imply that airlines only hire crew who embody perfect figures and harbour model looks. This is, quite frankly, utter nonsense. While there is no denying that airlines require candidates to be well groomed and portray a polished image, this element is usually taken out of context and to the extreme.

Appearance only matters in so far that you need to be within a healthy height to weight ratio, be well groomed and have no visible tattoos or piercings. It really is that simple.

And if the models in this book or on airlines websites concern you, those are just models whose job it is to look perfect,. Not to mention that they have been airbrushed to the max. It is simply marketing, and not reality.

Don't believe me? Think back to flights you have experienced or go check out the social media sites to see for yourself. Crew come in all shapes, sizes and appearances.

Dress Code

The good news
Emirates have a very defined dress code.

The bad news
Emirates have a very defined dress code.

While it is great that you don't' need to agonise about what to wear on your big day, this is also a bad thing because, with everyone dressed the same way, faces begin to blur and it is difficult to stand out.

This is why it is essential that you prepare and make the very best impression through your actions and how you approach the process.

The following sections will help you achieve this.

Before you go on, please take a moment to review the dress code on Emirates Group Careers page.

http://www.emiratesgroupcareers.com/cabin-crew/

Create a Memorable Impression

When faced with hundreds, and possibly thousands, of other candidates, merely creating a good impression just isn't enough. You need to be memorable. The trouble is, very few people know how to truly differentiate themselves from the competition. Most candidates enter the interview in their own little bubble, thinking that they only need to dress well and sell their skills and experience. Unfortunately, this is only a small part of it.

Creating a memorable impression goes far beyond what you wear and how you carry yourself, and even beyond the skills and experience you posses. In fact, it is so rare that only 2% of candidates ever make it through to being hired.

The secret to creating a memorable impression will surprise you in its simplicity, and yet many candidates are unaware that such an advantage even exists, let alone know how to evoke it. They often enter the process only prepared for the hard sell, if they are prepared at all, and end up merely blending in with the rest of the crowd.

Recruiters see this same thing time and time again, so any candidate who is prepared to put in just that little bit of extra effort will naturally stand out, and it is these candidates who, ultimately, get hired.

So what is this mysterious phenomenon and how can you use it to your advantage?

The Art of the Connection

This technique is actually not mysterious at all. In fact, it is not even a secret. The technique involves creating a connection or, most commonly referred to as, establishing a rapport. Rapport is such a powerful tool, as it is the quickest way to achieve a sensation of familiarity and trust between you and the recruiter. It is so powerful, in fact, that it can even sway the hiring decision in your favour.

Why does this technique work so well? Have you ever met someone for the first time and yet you felt a strong connection, just as if you'd known him or her forever? This is rapport in action. If you can establish this level of rapport with the recruiter or undercover officers, you can be sure they will remember you favourably.

MIRROR MIRROR

Mirroring is a process whereby you match your communication style, posture and mannerisms to those of another person. It is something you do naturally when you are deep in rapport with another person and is created by a deep feeling of unity. Using it consciously can evoke the sensation that the two of you are very much in sync just as readily as if it had occurred at a subconscious level, only you can be in control and use it to your own advantage.

As a note of caution, mirroring is something that must be done subtly to be effective. As such, it is important not to match every movement and not to react instantly to every change, else your motives will become obvious and the effectiveness of the technique will be lost.

For seamless results, take note of the following guidelines

Communication Style

Mirroring communication style can be done through using similar words or phrases, matching the sensory style, or mimicking the pitch, tempo and volume of their voice.

✈ Words and Phrases
We can make a fantastic psychological impact simply by injecting the recruiters own terminology and sequence of words into our answers. For example, if the interviewer points out that they are looking for and value a

candidate who is 'team spirited, customer focused and efficient', simply stating that we are 'good with customers, work well in a team and always make an effort', while implying the same values, will not create the same strong psychological impact.

➤ Pitch, Tempo and Volume
Matching our pitch, tempo and volume to the recruiters speaking style will make us appear in tune to what they are saying. This will speed up the rapport process and greatly improve our chances of creating a favourable impression.

➤ Sensory Style
While we all use a mix of the sensory styles: Visual, kinaesthetic and auditory, we tend to have a dominant style that we gravitate towards. If, during the course of the interview, it becomes obvious that the recruiter has a preference towards a particular sensory style, you can adjust your style accordingly to establish a deeper connection.

Visual people prefer to see how things are done rather than just talk about them. They are neat and orderly and take pride in their appearance. They speak rather quickly and use words that reflect their visual style, such as: 'I see what you mean', 'It looks to me like...', 'I imagine that...'

Auditory people like to use their voice and can easily go into lengthy discussions. They enjoy reading aloud and will often talk to themselves while working. Their style can be identified by their medium pace of speech and use of hearing words, such as: 'I hear what you are saying', 'We'll discuss this further', 'I hear you loud and clear'

Kinaesthetic people are very physically orientated and like to move a lot. They have difficultly sitting for long periods and use lots of expressive gestures as they speak. Their style can be identified by their slow pace and use of action words, such as: 'It feels as if...', 'It slipped my mind', 'I have a solid grasp...'

Next time you are in a public place, observe how people who appear to be closely connected do these same things. You could even try this out for yourself next time you are out for lunch with a close friend or family member. In fact, because this technique can appear uncomfortable and awkward the first time you try it, practicing will, in time, make it almost natural and automatic, and you may even find that your relationships begin to blossom more than usual.

Movements

✈ Matching and mirroring

When people have a strong connection with one another, they will subconsciously copy each other's body language. To quickly create a strong connection with the recruiter, the same technique may be applied.

As you are speaking with the recruiter, make a mental note of how they are sitting and what they are doing with their hands. Then, subtly mirror their position and gestures. If they are leaning forward, you might lean forward also. If they have their hands clasped on the table, you might do the same.

The key to successfully utilising this technique is subtlety. If we become obvious by reacting instantly to each and every change, the effectiveness of the technique will be lost. Similarly, if we mirror closed signals, we may accomplish only a negative connection.

The best time to mirror a position is when we engage in dialogue. For example: The recruiter leans forward as they begin to ask a question. As we engage our follow up response, a change in position would appear natural and go completely unnoticed.

✈ Leading

Leading is an influencing technique which can be used to judge the level of connection. For example: If you feel you have achieved rapport with the recruiter and both of you have your hands in your lap and are sat up straight, you could lean forward slightly and clasp your hands gently onto the table. If the recruiter follows your lead, you can be sure that you have established a strong connection.

Disconnection

It is important to be perceptive to signs that the recruiter has become disconnected so that we can be proactive in re-establishing a connection.

Before attempting to reconnect, however, it is important to establish the accuracy of our perceptions because we may have simply misread the signal or it could be a by-product of our paranoid imagination. Similarly, the perceived signal may be a momentary motion that has no substance or it may be unrelated to us entirely.

To reliably determine the accuracy of our observation, we first need to scan for clusters of signals that are supportive of our perception. If we observe two or more congruent signals, this is a definite cluster. Next, we can test our connection by attempting to 'lead' (see above). If the recruiter doesn't follow, this is also a sure sign that a disconnection has taken place.

Disconnection Signals Include:

✈ Fake smile
✈ Closed gestures
✈ Using barriers
✈ Directing their body away
✈ Writing notes
✈ Fidgeting

✈ Yawning
✈ Stretching
✈ Shifting
✈ Tidying the desk
✈ Slouching

Disapproval Signals Include:

- ✈ Pursed lips
- ✈ Eye squinting
- ✈ Jaw clenching
- ✈ Licking lips
- ✈ Rubbing eyes

- ✈ Frowning
- ✈ Increased blinking rate
- ✈ Shaking head
- ✈ Scratching

When to use it

During the group stages, you will not have an opportunity to forge any kind of connection with the official recruiters, however, you will be up close and very personal with the undercover team and it is here that you will be focusing much of your attention during these early stages.

The trouble is, how do you know who is undercover and who is a candidate? Unfortunately ,you don't. As such, the only possible way to accomplish this task is to make this same effort with every candidate you meet. While this may seem like an arduous and inefficient task, your efforts will pay off many times over, as you will gain an advantage like no other. In the worst instance, you will come away with a few new friends.

During the latter stages of the final interview, you can refocus your efforts on the official recruiters. This is where the technique will really come into its own and you can use it to its full advantage.

The One Type Who Always Gets the Job

As you can now see, there is always one type who gets the job offer, but it isn't the best looking one as myths and legend would have you believe. The simple truth is that recruiters hire those individuals that they personally like and feel a connection with.

The biggest mistake most candidates make is that they enter the interview focused only on themselves and miss any opportunity to make a connection. A candidate who makes an effort will not only come across as more genuine and sincere, they will also instantly differentiate themselves from the competition, so it is certainly worthwhile putting the extra effort into perfecting this technique.

Just Like Old Friends

Another trick, which can be used as an adjunct to the previous technique, is to think of the recruiter as a good friend. Now I am not suggesting you take this literally, or you risk appearing too informal and familiar, what I am suggesting is that you enter the interview in a natural and conversational frame of mind.

The point of this technique is to help you relax, but also to assist the interviewer in breaking the ice. Simply initiating some friendly dialogue as you first meet the recruiter will help you to create an aura of a warm and approachable person, but also one who is relaxed and confident. Such a personable approach can help the interviewer feel more comfortable in your presence and will certainly get the interview off to a great start.

Naturally you will want to use common sense here to avoid stepping over the invisible line, however, it is important to remember that most candidates will only be thinking about themselves. The interviewer will appreciate your effort to connect.

The Enthusiastic Approach

If there is just one more thing that can set one candidate apart from the rest, it is the expression of a sincere passion and enthusiasm for the job, airline and the opportunity. Sadly, many people believe that showing enthusiasm will be mistaken for desperation and, as such, suppress their enthusiasm in favour of the laid back and relaxed approach. The truth is, the laid back approach is often mistaken for indifference or disinterest, and this can severely hinder your chances of success.

Another misconception is that being enthusiastic means that you need to be loaded with energy and bouncing off the walls. This is bordering on excitement, rather than enthusiasm, and is not ideal either. As discussed previously, the idea is to match the tempo of the person you are speaking to, and injecting too much energy can make it difficult for others to relate and connect with you, not to mention exhausting. You can certainly be calm and still be enthusiastic.

So what exactly is enthusiasm and how can you use it appropriately?

Use it appropriately

There are several ways that you can display your enthusiasm. This could be through an eagerness and willingness to learn, your facial expression and smile, an expression of pride in your work, actively listening and asking questions, taking notes and even through your knowledge and research about the opportunity and the airline.

You can also be upfront about your enthusiasm by stating it directly. For instance, when asked "Why do you want to be cabin crew?", speak from the heart as you tell them your personal story and the steps you have been taking to achieve your dream. If you have a sincere passion for meeting people from different cultures, express it. If you have a genuine love for assisting in the comfort of others, use it. If you have been participating in volunteer work to enhance your skills for the position, tell them. This is truly where you will stand head over heels above the run-of-the-mill answers that they hear 95% of the time.

Don't underestimate the power

It sounds simple, and even, superfluous, when compared to tangible skills and experiences, however, do not underestimate the power of honest and sincere enthusiasm. It is contagious and will energise those around you. More importantly, recruiters will pick up on your positive energy and will sense that you will approach the job with vigour.

Consider your communication

Because effective communication skills are essential for interview success, it is important to be mindful of how our communication is received. This means that we must consider not only the words we use, but also how our tonality and body language complement or contradict those words.

Consider the following communication guidelines:

Word Choice

Words are important because they communicate and convey our message succinctly. So, even at a low 7% accountability, our word choice can mean the difference between a powerful, captivating and influential exchange, and a weak, disempowering and ineffective one. To create the desired response, consider the following guidelines:

✈ Action Words
Action words are positive, powerful and directive, and should be used abundantly. Action words include: Communicated, conveyed, directed, listened, persuaded, arranged, handled and improved.

✈ Filler Words
Anyways, you know how when you are, like, really nervous, and you ,ummm, find it hard to verbalise and stuff, and you say silly things that, kind of, make you sound, like, kind of, unprofessional and maybe, like, inarticulate?

The useless and annoying verbal mannerisms used in the above example "you know," "like," "in other words," "kind of," "ummm," and "anyways." should be avoided at all costs. Besides sounding unprofessional, they also distract attention from the message.

✈ Undermining Words
Words and phrases such as 'I think,' 'I hope,' 'maybe,' 'sort of,' 'perhaps,' 'I guess,' all undermine your message and credibility by creating the impression that you don't trust your own knowledge or opinion. Eliminating these phrases will drastically improve the quality of any message.

✈ Jargon, Slang and Clichés
Specialist terminology and informal expressions can confuse an outside audience. Avoid these where possible, and stick to simple, clear and coherent language.

Tonality

Our tonality plays a key role in sending the correct messages. So, if our aim is to project confidence, enthusiasm and expertise, it is important to exercise control and awareness of our tonality throughout our interactions.

✈ Pitch
Pitch refers to the degree of highness and lowness in our voice. A variation in our pitch creates meaning, adds clarity and makes what we are saying more interesting. For instance: A rise in our pitch suggests we are asking a question, which indicates doubt, uncertainty and hesitation. A fall in pitch indicates a statement, which further suggests certainty and assurance.

✈ Tempo
Tempo refers to the speed of our voice. If we speak too slowly, we risk losing the interest and attention of our audience. If we speak too fast, others may find us difficult to follow. The key is to maintain a pace which is fast enough to maintain interest, yet slow enough to be clear.

✈ Volume

Volume refers to the loudness of our voice. Speaking in a loud volume suggests aggression, while a quiet volume indicates shyness and makes it difficult to be heard. The key to determining the appropriate volume is to keep your voice loud enough to be heard, but soft enough to be clear. Modulation of volume can also be introduced to keep the speech interesting and add extra emphasis.

✈ Articulation

Articulation refers to our vocal clarity. Regardless of our pitch, tempo, volume and accent, we need to make a conscious effort to enunciate clearly.

Body Language

The way we carry ourselves, the gestures we use and our facial expressions communicate all sorts of messages, so learning to control certain aspects of these can help us to convey the message of a well-balanced, confident individual.

We use open gestures when we are feeling confident and relaxed, and are being honest and sincere. Therefore, to be perceived as relaxed, sincere and confident, keep your arms unfolded, your legs uncrossed and your palms open.

Gesturing can also be useful for adding emphasis to what we are saying and, if the movements we employ are subtle and controlled, it is perfectly okay to use gestures to express ourselves and endorse our words. For best results, keep any movements below shoulder level, but above the waistline.

If you find your movements become excessive or distracting, simply rest your hands on the table or loosely in your lap.

✦ Open Palms

Open palms signify honesty and give the impression of a relaxed and confident person.

✦ Steepling fingers

This gesture is understood to be a sign of confidence and authority.

✦ Nodding

Nodding your head in agreement when the recruiter is speaking will signal that you are listening and understand. However, be careful not to over emphasise the movement.

Top 10 negative gestures

✦ Finger Pointing
✦ Karate Chopping
✦ Hand Wringing
✦ Feet Tapping
✦ Pen Clicking

✦ Fist Pounding
✦ Finger Drumming
✦ Oversized Gestures
✦ Arm Crossing
✦ Hair Twirling

Posture

To portray the image of a confident and motivated person, adopt an upright and attentive posture that is open, yet relaxed. Keep your chin parallel to the floor, shoulders back and spine straight.

If seated, lean slightly forward with your hands loosely in your lap, or on the table. Place both feet flat on the floor, or cross your ankles.

If standing, keep your arms loosely at your side or behind your back and plant your feet about 8-10 inches apart. If standing for long periods, place one foot slightly in front of the other to allow you to smoothly and unnoticeably shift weight between your feet.

Facial Expressions

Our facial expressions convey a wide range of attitudes, feelings and emotions, and these can have a significant impact on our ability to connect with others. Because of this, it is important to be aware of the story our face is telling and work to convey an attentive, sincere and interested expression.

A positive expression can certainly include a smile, but doesn't necessarily imply its inclusion. In fact, maintaining a constant smile is not only uncomfortable, it is also completely unnecessary. Instead, an open expression that includes a gentle and understated smile, soft eyes and slightly elevated eyebrows will result in a soft and pleasant expression.

Large smiles should be reserved for introductions and the occasional injection during conversation.

Handshake

Your hand shake says a lot about you. A firm handshake conveys confidence, assertiveness and professionalism. A weak, limp handshake suggests shyness and insecurity, and a strong, crushing handshake indicates aggression and dominance.

To perform a professional and confident handshake, follow these simple guidelines:

Before connecting for the handshake establish eye contact, smile and lean slightly forward. As you extend your right hand, keep your hand straight and thumb pointing upwards. When your hands connect engage a firm, but not crushing, grip. Shake one to three times, for a duration of 1-3 seconds, and break away.

Eye Contact

Good eye contact is one of the most important factors of body language. Shifty eyes, or complete avoidance of contact can suggest dishonesty, boredom, rudeness, insecurity or shyness.

If you find eye contact anxiety provoking and uncomfortable, direct your gaze at their eyebrows, forehead, or bridge of the nose. This is not a permanent solution by any means, but it will certainly ease you into the process.

In an attempt to forge eye contact, be aware not to stare as this can indicate aggression and make others feel uncomfortable. To avoid this extreme, lighten your gaze and keep it friendly. This can be achieved by allowing your eyes to go slightly out of focus.

If you have notes, you can temporarily break eye contact as you refer to these. Also, f there is a second recruitment officer present, this will give you another opportunity to break eye contact as you periodically direct your focus back and forth between the two.

Eye Accessing Cues

As with our facial expressions, our eyes reveal much about how we are feeling. This could be through our eye contact, blink rate, or eye movements.

We blink, on average, 10 times per minute. When we are relaxed, our blink rate reflects this slower rate. When we are anxious, uncomfortable or being dishonest, our blink rate increases.

Our eye movements, eye accessing cues, reveal whether we are accessing a memory, or constructing one. While it is debated as to whether we can catch someone lying by watching their eye direction, we can certainly determine what sensory system they are accessing.

✈ VC - Visual Constructed
This would be the direction a persons eyes moved in when they are constructing new visual images.

✈ AC - Auditory Constructed
This would be the direction a persons eyes moved in when they 'auditory construct' a sound in their mind.

✈ K - Kinaesthetic
This would be the direction a persons eyes move in as they recall a smell, feeling or taste.

✈ VR - Visual Remembered
This would be the direction a persons eyes moved in when they are visually remembering the past.

✈ AR - Auditory Remembered
This would be the direction a persons eyes moved in when they are remembering sounds from the past.

✈ AD - Auditory Digital
This would be the direction a persons eyes moved in when they access internal dialogue

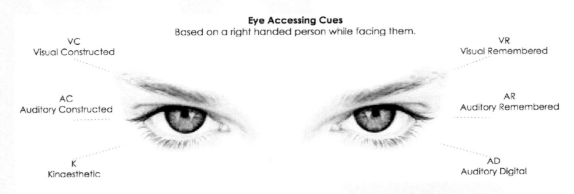

Eye Accessing Cues
Based on a right handed person while facing them.

VC
Visual Constructed

VR
Visual Remembered

AC
Auditory Constructed

AR
Auditory Remembered

K
Kinaesthetic

AD
Auditory Digital

Communication Barriers

Barriers to effective communication may arise for a number of reasons. When these barriers do occur, we are forced to become even more effective in our ability to communicate. The strategies below will help overcome some of these more effectively.

✈ Language
Language barriers are a common challenge in interview settings. If you struggle with the native language of the airline, or have a very strong accent, speak slowly and clearly, ask for clarification and check for understanding, avoid idioms and jargon, use gestures and be specific, listen actively and be patient.

✈ Cultural
Because every culture has its own set of values, beliefs and behaviours, the potential for confusion and misunderstanding is high. Even when we speak the same language, these differences can lead to challenges. To effectively connect with an individual from a culturally different background, it is important to be sensitive and respectful, avoid prejudice and stereotyping, and be aware of using questionable language and gestures.

✈ Gender
Barriers in communication between genders exist primarily because men and women have different communication patterns. To overcome these barriers, it is important to appreciate, learn and understand the different strengths and styles that exist.

While men tend to be more direct and factual, women tend to be indirect and tactful. Men have a preference for reason and logic, are competitive and are interested in power, rank and status. Women are empathetic and feeling oriented. They value relationships and like to build rapport. Men communicate to exchange information and solve problems, while women communicate to share and a build connection.

✈ Emotional

Emotional barriers within an interview situation manifest themselves through fear, shyness or restraint. When we feel distracted by these emotional states, our ability to communicate at an effective level is severely inhibited. We may wrongly interpret the actions and words of others, and may not effectively express our own opinion. We may even stop listening to the other person as our internal dialogue takes over.

Master the Art of Small Talk

Recruiters recognise that job interviews are nerve wracking events and will usually open the session with a brief period of small talk. Perhaps this is an attempt to merely break the ice, or possibly a way to judge your communication and people skills while under pressure. Either way, your involvement can have a direct impact on your overall success and consideration for your responses should be given.

To help you successfully navigate your way through the minefield of interview small talk, I have prepared the following guidelines.

✈ Stick to safe topics

Keep your focus on positive or neutral topics such as the weather and traffic. Discussions about politics or religion should be avoided, as should negative or controversial current events. Each of these can stir up some very strong emotions and shift the interview in a negative direction very quickly.

✈ Show interest

While discussions about the weather and traffic are not particularly engaging, an effort should be made to look interested.

✈ Give short responses

Small talk should remain small. Long winded stories about the journey, the weather, or the latest sports news are not only unnecessary, they are also inappropriate. Respond in a conversational tone, but don't get carried away.

✈ Be sincere

Being friendly too quickly or being overly complimentary may appear desperate and insincere. To be effective, keep pleasantries minimal and sincere.

✈ Be positive

There is no room for negativity of any kind. Even if you had trouble finding the location or got stuck in a long traffic jam on your way to the venue, a positive response is the only one that should be considered.

For instance:

"How was your journey?"
"Very well, thank you"
"I hope the traffic wasn't too terrible?"
"I expected a little traffic, so I left early for this reason"
"Did you find the venue okay?"
"Yes, thank you. I found your map to be a great help"

Control your body language
Even during this seemingly informal discussion, our body language is important. Convey a professional and confident message by maintaining steady eye contact, keeping an upright posture and wearing a warm smile.

PART FOUR
ATTEND

NAIL THE
GROUP INTERVIEW

What to Expect

The assessment process varies considerably in length and structure as these processes are often updated.

Since Emirates closed recruitment in 2016, the whole process has been going through a major restructure and the process is being kept under wraps until recruitment reopens. As such, the guidelines below are only accurate based on what has happened previously and are subject to change. These guidelines will be updated as information is released.

Open days typically attract a high volume of candidates and, as such, will often be split over a series of days, however, open days have now been eliminated in favour of the video pre-screening process covered in a previous section. Invitation only days are kept much smaller in number and may span only a few short hours with final interviews conducted the following day or at a later date.

In either case, you will be asked to partake is a number of activities. These activities are designed to reveal your personality, competencies and potential for working as cabin crew and are likely to include a series of individual assessments, practical tasks, group discussions and role-play scenarios.

Arrival at the event can seem overwhelming, especially when faced with hundreds of applicants in attendance. You will likely be met with an atmosphere that is friendly and buzzing with adrenaline, but has an eerie sense of tension, as each candidate is anxious to get through the process. This atmosphere generally tapers off as the sessions get underway.

The Icebreaker

The recruitment personnel will often start the day with a short introductory briefing and a breakdown of the intended days events. This session should last no more than 30 minutes or so, and allows for any remaining candidates to arrive before the event officially gets underway.

The icebreaker session may involve a short presentation about the airline followed by an open discussion session. During this time, candidates are encouraged to pose questions to the personnel about the airline and the position.

This session can be tricky because it's easy to stand out for all the wrong reasons.

If a question is asked that has already been answered within the airline literature, this will highlight a lack of prior research. A question that requires a lengthy answer will either annoy the recruiters or they will decline to answer, and that's never a good thing.

You'll also find that many of the more confident candidates make the mistake of getting carried away with their line of questioning in an attempt to stand out. Unfortunately, asking too many questions at this stage will only demonstrate a general lack of respect for others, who also have questions, and is also more likely to be misconstrued as arrogant, rather than confident.

If there's one tip I can give you, it's to bear in mind that this is only an icebreaker session. The recruitment personnel don't want to be answering a long list of questions and neither do they want to be giving long answers to complicated questions, so if you do want to ask a question, ask only ONE question, keep it brief and simple to answer.

And remember, you don't need to ask a question if you don't have one suitable. There will be plenty of opportunities to stand out as the day goes on. It's better to remain silent here than risk asking the wrong question.

So, what question should you ask? There are three types of questions that work well within this scenario, these are:

✈ Questions that demonstrate your research about the airline and the position
✈ Questions that highlight your enthusiasm
✈ Questions that reflect some depth to your motives

But honestly, each of these types of questions have the potential to require long-winded responses or may put the recruiter too much into the spotlight to perform. During this stage, I'd only ask a question if it is expected of you or you have a burning question that hasn't been answered through any prior means.

Self Introduction

You may be asked to give a short introduction about yourself and this my friend is where you can truly shine.

As well as learning more about you and your background, these self-introductions are an opportunity for the recruiters to assess how well you cope when addressing a group of people and how articulately you are able to communicate your message while under pressure. In their assessment, they will be looking for good delivery and a certain amount of charisma.

To deliver a self-introduction that makes an impact, here are some guidelines for you to consider.

✈ Make it relevant
Use this opportunity to highlight your suitability for the job of cabin crew by sharing interesting facts about your present or most recent job, and your motives for making a career change.

✈ Be spontaneous
A self-presentation which is spontaneous, rather than rehearsed, will add life and sincerity to your speech. Sure you can prepare a rough draft and familiarise yourself with it, but don't try to learn it by heart, as there is a risk of appearing forced, dull and robotic.

✈ Inject personality
Show your passion and enthusiasm by injecting some emotion and personality into your presentation.

✈ Be concise
Unless advised otherwise, keep it relatively short and focused. Thirty to Sixty seconds should be sufficient.

✈ Rotate your focus

To give the impression of confidence and engage your audience, rotate your gaze and make eye contact with various members for three to five seconds each, then be sure to redirect your focus back to the recruiters to finish your presentation.

✈ Beware of how you sound

Varying your tone, pitch, volume and pace will eliminate the risk of appearing monotone and make it enjoyable for others to listen to. If you are nervous, you may be more inclined to rush. It will help if you make a deliberate attempt to slow your pace slightly.

✈ Consider this example

" Hi everyone. My name is Caitlyn and it's really nice to meet you all. I'm 27 years old and live in the bustling city of Bristol. I currently work as a personal trainer, which is a job I really enjoy, but I have always wanted to be cabin crew with ___ airlines because of it's fun corporate culture and innovative approaches to travel, which is why I am here today. I hope I can bring some pizazz of my own"

What are they looking for?

This is the one question I am asked, time and time again. So many candidates overanalyse the process, but the answer is actually very simple. So simple in fact that most of you you will already know what I am going to say.

The recruiters are assessing six key competencies. These are:

✈ Communication skills   ✈ Customer focus
✈ Leadership   ✈ Interpersonal ability
✈ Team spirit   ✈ Initiative

And of course, your match with the corporate culture.

In order to determine these competencies, the assessors will be observing the following aspects:

✈ Your level of participation and interaction
✈ Your behaviour towards the activities and your peers
✈ Your communication and work style
✈ Your ability to think on your feet and react to external pressure
✈ Your ability to lead and willingness to follow

Corporate Culture

As you already discovered in a previous section, corporate culture is a very important aspect that is always being assessed throughout your interactions and involvement in the group tasks. For this reason, you should always assume that no matter how irrelevant a task may appear, there is always an underlying motive for its inclusion, and you can almost always be sure it is being sized up against this important criteria.

The confusion

Group tasks are designed so that assessors can view and assess these core competencies first hand, and how you behave during each task will be taken as a clear indication of how you may perform in reality.

While it goes without saying that how you behave during an interview is not going to be an accurate representation when compared with a real life scenario, it is through your involvement and behaviour, that assessors can identify positive and negative attributes first hand and be able to make better decisions.

Where most individuals often become confused is between the relevancy of the task and what is actually being observed.

Because some of the tasks bear no obvious relevance to the cabin crew role, it is easy to overlook the underlying motives and get caught up in the practicalities of the task instead. And herein lies the trick: The outcome of the task itself is irrelevant.

This is so important that it bears repeating. The outcome of the task itself is irrelevant. Let me explain this further....

Assessors are more concerned with how well you perform under pressure and in a team environment, how you communicate your ideas, how you interact with others and what role you assume than they are to see if you can decide your way out of being trapped on a desert island.

When you think back to the group tasks you have participated in, do you notice that they appear to have no right or wrong answer? That's because there is no right or wrong answer.

As an example, consider the following popular group topic:

Topic:

The plane has gone down over the Atlantic Ocean. There are eight survivors, but the one surviving life raft only has a capacity for four people. As a team, identify four survivors from the following list who you would save and state your reasons why. Select a spokesperson to present your decision and explain why you came up with the answer.

✈ You (the flight attendant)   ✈ An ex army general
✈ A pregnant lady   ✈ A world class athlete
✈ The pope   ✈ A surgeon
✈ A child   ✈ A nurse

Clearly there is no right answer to this topic, as you wouldn't want to decide such a fate for four people and the recruiters understand that such a decision would be difficult. So what is the point of this task?

Take another look at the topic and notice the words I have emphasised are 'team' and 'present'. These are the keys to this task.

Assessors are looking to observe how you interact as part of a team, and whether you demonstrate initiative and leadership by volunteering to present the information back to the rest of the group. Most candidates will focus on everything except for those two key points.

Let's take a look at another example: Singing.

Many candidates understand the concept of a discussion or role-play scenario, but just do not understand how singing bears any relevance. Again, this is very simple to comprehend if you read between the lines and understand the motives.

Task:

Tasks haven't been a typical part of Emirates selection process in the past, however things are always being updated and new approaches included, so it is always best to be prepared for everything. As such, I'll go through a couple of sample tasks below that you may encoutner as part of a cabin crew selection process.

Many passengers ignore safety demonstrations because they feel they have heard it all before. In an effort to increase safety, Emirates Airlines is considering an overhaul of its safety procedures. As a team, come up with a new safety demonstration, which will encourage passengers to pay attention to these important briefings.

The demonstration can include appropriate humour, and must be sung according to the melody given to you on the back of the card. The outcome should be no more than 5 minutes in length and each individual must play a role in the final presentation.

Within this task, you can see that team is once again emphasised, but the additional mention of a deadline and that each individual must participate tells us that your ability to follow the instructions and stick to the schedule is being observed, as is your own ability to take part.

Because the task focuses on singing, you can be sure the airline wants to see if you are willing to let go and have fun.

Whatever task you are asked to participte in, you can be sure that the airline is sizing you up against its corporate culture and, if you feel too modest to participate, you may want to reassess the corporate culture is suitable with your own style.

Even if you feel utterly silly and have the worst voice in the world, you should be standing confident as if you are Celine Dion or Christina Aguilera during this task because you can be sure that's what the recruiters want to see. In fact, having a bad voice can stand you in good stead during this task because you'll make people smile if you give it your best effort.

Make em smile and you'll bag that job.

Tips for Standing Out

✈ Have fun
However silly or irrelevant the tasks may seem, your active involvement is essential. So, rather than concern yourself about external details, just relax and allow yourself to enjoy the process. This positive viewpoint will reflect well on your character, demonstrate enthusiasm, and make the experience a fun filled one for you.

✈ Contribute
Contributing ideas and making suggestions is another great way to demonstrate your enthusiasm and team spirit. It will show that you are able to express yourself and are keen to get involved.

✈ Volunteer

There are times when no candidate wants to put their neck on the line, so volunteering is a great way to demonstrate your enthusiasm and it will show that you are not afraid to take the initiative.

✈ Use names

Remembering people's names will demonstrate your ability to listen and pay attention to detail. Moreover, it will demonstrate a tremendous amount of respect for others and create a lasting impact.

✈ Summarise

Summarising the main points of a discussion is a great way to move past awkward moments of silence and sticking points. The breathing room summarising creates will typically stimulate further ideas and encourage participation. Not only will your peers be grateful for the momentary relief, your communication and leadership ability will also be highlighted.

✈ Be positive

When you choose to exhibit a positive spirit, people will naturally be drawn towards your character. So, be enthusiastic about the exercises you are asked to undertake and be encouraging towards others.

✈ Be encouraging

If any members of your team remain reserved, encourage their involvement by asking if they have an idea, suggestion or opinion. This shows empathy, consideration and team spirit. This is such a great quality to demonstrate, and one that is often missed by over-zealous candidates.

✈ Support the leader

If you have one or more powerful characters in your team who have stepped up to the leadership position, show your support in helping them to succeed within that role. Just because a team has a leader, doesn't mean everyone else should fall by the wayside. Showing support will show the ultimate team spirit.

...And what to avoid

✈ Over involvement
Getting involved and showing enthusiasm in a task is fantastic, but over involvement and incessant talking can leave others struggling to get involved and may transfer across to assessors as arrogance. Always provide others with an opportunity to provide their opinion.

✈ Under involvement
For assessors to make an informed assessment, active involvement from each individual is essential. Those who are unable to get involved, for whatever reason, will surely be eliminated.

✈ Entering into a dispute
Conflicting views are natural, however, a group assessment is neither the time or place to engage in a hostile dispute with other candidates.

✈ Criticising
Even if your intentions are honourable and the feedback is constructive, criticising another candidates opinions, actions and ideas may be perceived as an attack. An assessment day is neither the time nor the place.

✈ Being negative
Making negative remarks or exhibiting frustration over tasks, peers or previous employers , no matter how harmless it may seem, will raise serious concerns about your attitude and ethics.

✈ Being bossy
There is nothing wrong with striving for excellence, however, being dominant and imposing your ideas on others is overbearing and intimidating. This always leads others to feel incompetent.

✈ Not listening or talking over others
Neglecting to listen to instructions leads to misinterpretations and displays a general lack of enthusiasm. Not listening or talking over others is ignorant and disrespectful.

Get Involved...

I know it goes without saying, and I've covered this briefly above, but it bears repeating that it is only through your active involvement that recruiters are able to assess your suitability and identify your positive attributes. So however silly or irrelevant the tasks may seem, or how difficult it is to get your opinion across, your involvement is essential.

Rather than concern yourself about external details, just relax and allow yourself to enjoy the process. This positive viewpoint will reflect well on your character, demonstrate enthusiasm, and make the experience a fun filled one for you.

I understand that it can be difficult to get involved when you are in a group of individuals who have big personalities. They set off on a tangent, leaving you feeling like you are on the outside struggling to get in. While these conditions do pose a difficult challenge, it is absolutely essential that you do what you can to be included. Raise your hand if you need to, but whatever you do, don't remain on the outside.

If you suffer from nervousness, understand that it is okay to be nervous, even permissible, but allowing your nerves to keep you from getting involved is not. It is better to risk displaying your nerves than it is to remain silent. At least the recruiters will appreciate your effort.

...But don't overdo it

Getting involved and showing enthusiasm in a task is fantastic, but over involvement and incessant talking can leave others struggling to get involved and may transfer across to assessors as arrogance.

f you do notice that other members of your team remain reserved or appear to be struggling to get involved, encourage their involvement by asking if they have an idea, suggestion or opinion. This is a clear indication of empathy, consideration and team spirit and it is these qualities that recruiters will be impressed by.

Role Play Scenarios

Role-play scenarios may be performed with other candidates as a pair or within a group. The scenarios will bear some relation to the demands of the job and are likely to include:

✈ Intoxicated passenger
✈ Terrorist threat
✈ Toilet smoker
✈ Fearful passenger
✈ Disorderly behaviour
✈ Disruptive child
✈ Abusive behaviour
✈ Passenger complaint

The assessors don't expect you to know the answer to every possible scenario they introduce. They simply want to see how you react in challenging situations. So, when taking part in any role play scenario, use the following guidelines:

✈ Be proactive and do your best to resolve the situation using your initiative
✈ Remain calm and composed
✈ Be direct and assertive e
✈ Immerse yourself into the role
✈ Take each scenario seriously
✈ Devise a plan and follow it as much as possible
✈ Have fun

Here are some pointers to help you deal with some common scenarios:

✈ Passenger Complaint:
In the case of a passenger complaint, it is important that you listen to their concern without interruption. Ask questions, where appropriate, to clarify their concerns and show empathy towards their situation. If the facts warrant it, apologise for the situation, explain what action you intend to take and thank them for bringing the matter to your attention.

✈ Scared Passenger
If a passenger is fearful of flying, be considerate of their feelings. Use a gentle and calm tone to talk them through the flight and reassure them of any sounds or sensations they may experience. Let the passenger know where you can be found and show them the call bell.

✈ Intoxicated Passenger
Offer the passenger a cup of tea or coffee and don't provide any more alcoholic drinks. You could also encourage the passenger to eat some food. Remain calm towards the passenger, but be direct and assertive in your approach. If you feel it appropriate, inform your senior and seek assistance from other crew members.

Common Concerns

Being Alienated

When there are a lot of different personalities in a group and the emotions are high, it can become difficult to get involved. This is especially true during a large group discussion. In these instances, you should employ some of the following strategies for getting your voice heard.

✈ Raise your hand
As simple as it seems, raising your hand will demand the attention of the group and let them know that you have something to say.

✈ Be assertive
If raising your hand reaps no results, you will have to be more assertive. Wait for a momentary pause in the conversation, and simple say "excuse me" before proceeding. This may feel uncomfortable for some of you, but it is imperative that you contribute. If done calmly and respectfully, the assessors will be impressed by your effort.

Handling Disagreements

If you disagree with an approach being taken by the group or an idea which has been brought forth, it is perfectly reasonable to say so as long as you are constructive and positive in doing so. Consider the following statements:

✈ Negative:
"That wouldn't work. I think we should..."

✈ Constructive
"I see your point, Mark, but there are a number of issues that may arise with that approach. How about we consider..."
The former example attacks and ridicules the idea, while the latter demonstrates a positive acknowledgement before a new idea is introduced. In the instance that your new idea is rejected, remain polite and seek input from the group. If you are clearly outnumbered, gracefully accept the decision and move on.

Being Ridiculed

If your idea is ridiculed, resist the temptation to retaliate. Instead, remain cordial and respectful in your response. This graceful reaction will be duly noted and respected by the assessors.

Feeling Uncertain

You don't always have to give an opinion when you speak. Supporting what someone else has said, asking a legitimate question, or commenting on an emerging theme are equally good ways to make your presence known without appearing as if you like the sound of your own voice.

Points to Consider

In most cases, the outcome of each task or topic is largely irrelevant. Assessors are more concerned with how well you perform in a team environment, how you communicate your ideas and interact with others, and what role you typically assume.

Thus, no matter how you feel, you should approach every task with a can do attitude and every topic in a calm and conversational tone.

Personality Tests

Through a series of simple questions, personality tests provide assessors with an indication of a candidates character, behaviour and work style. The test results merely supplement the recruiters own observations from the interview and, as such, there are no right or wrong answers.

Typical questions you will encounter are:

For each question, give a mark out of five.
One = Disagree strongly
Five = Agree strongly

✈ I enjoy meeting new people.
✈ I get bored with repetitive tasks.
✈ I often lose my temper when I am frustrated.
✈ I always think before I act.
✈ I work well under pressure.
✈ I find it easy to relax.
✈ I get on well with most people.
✈ I am a team player.
✈ I prefer to work alone.
✈ I become nervous in social situations.
✈ I find it difficult to communicate with other cultures.
✈ I thrive on challenges.

In an attempt to create a favourable impression, some candidates try to imagine how the recruiters want them to be and will answer questions dishonestly. I would advise against this strategy because any contradiction between your answers and the recruiters own observations will make it obvious that the answers have been embellished.

Language Proficiency Tests

If a second language is a requirement of the airline or if English isn't your native language, you may be required to complete a language assessment based on the following four key skills:

✈ Listening
✈ Reading
✈ Writing
✈ Speaking

Performance will be evaluated by how well the candidate understands and can be understood.

Listening

In this section of the test, you will have the chance to show how well you understand the spoken language. Questions you may come across are as follows:

✈ You will see a picture, and you will hear four short statements. When you hear the statements, look at the picture and choose the statement that best describes what you see in the picture.

✈ You will hear a question or statement, followed by three responses. You are to choose the best response to each question or statement. You will hear a short conversation between two people.

✈ You will then read a question about each conversation. The question will be followed by four answers. You are to choose the best answer to each question.

Reading

In this section of the test, you will have the chance to show how well you understand the written language.

Here are some examples:

Choose one word which best completes the following sentence.

Because the equipment is very delicate, it must be handled with _____.
(A) Caring (B) Careful (C) Care (D) Carefully

Identify one underlined word which should be corrected or rewritten.

All employees are repaired to wear their identification badges while at work.

(A) employees (B) repaired (C) wear (D) identification

Writing & Speaking

In the written and spoken sections of the test, you will have the chance to show how well you speak and write the language.

You may be asked basic questions about your home town, family, work or study, leisure and future plans.

Numerical Ability Test

Numeracy tests are designed to test your basic arithmetic skills: Addition, subtraction, multiplication and division. While they are typically short and relatively simple in nature, if you haven't exercised your maths brain for some time, it may be a good idea to practice some basic mental arithmetic before the interview.

Here are some sample questions to get your juices flowing.

Calculators may or may not be permitted.
1. What is Twelve Thousand Nine Hundred and Seventy Six in figures?
A. 129,76.00   B. 12,976,000   C. 12,976.00

2. What is 6 multiplied by 8?
A. 48 B. 52   C. 46

3. Add 67 to 12
A. 80   B. 79   C. 76

4. You begin with a float of 66.94. A customer purchases a pack of peanuts at 0.66, a shot of spirits at 3.54 and a pack of chewing gum at 0.53. How much float should you have following this transaction?
A. 62.21   B. 71.76   C. 71.67

5. There are 357 seats on your aircraft. The seats are divided into three cabins. How many seats are in each cabin?
A. 117   B. 119   C. 109

General Knowledge Quiz

General knowledge tests are fairly straightforward. The questions cover a broad range of topics and are likely to include political, geographical, historical, entertainment and scientific areas. Here are some sample test questions to give you a better idea of what to expect.

✈ In relation to time, what does the abbreviation GMT stand for?
✈ How many continents are there?
✈ What is the name of the highest mountain in the world?
✈ Which is the largest continent?
✈ What is the capital of the USA?
✈ In which country would you find the river Nile?
✈ In which continent would you find Russia?
✈ Who is the president of the United States?
✈ Where will the next Olympics be held?

NAIL THE
FINAL INTERVIEW

Congratulations if you have made it through to the final interview.

Having assessed your involvement and performance during the group sessions, the recruiters have clearly observed qualities in your character that they admire, and would now like to explore your motives further. So revel in the success you have achieved to this point, and be ready to close out this process.

During the final interview, the recruiters will seek to explore your motives for applying to the airline and your desire for pursuing a career as cabin crew. Moreover, they will seek to gather information about your work history, character and work ethic to determine whether you will fit the job and airline.

To ease you into the interview process, and make you feel more relaxed, the recruiters will typically open the session with questions about you and your background. They will then seek to explore your motivation for applying to the airline and making a career change. Questions such as "Why do you want to work for Emirates?" and "Why do you want to be cabin crew?" are common at this stage.

With the interview thoroughly under way, the recruiters will want to determine whether you possess the skills and experience necessary for the position. Here you can expect more probing situational and behavioural questions, such as "When have you handled a customer complaint?" and "Describe a time when you failed to communicate effectively".

Although there appears to be no typical duration for panel interviews, you can expect a baseline time of at least 20 minutes, to upwards of 1 hour or more. In either case, the duration has no bearing on your ultimate success; so do not overly concern yourself with this aspect. An interview lasting just 20 minutes doesn't indicate a failure, just as an interview in excess of 1 hour does not indicate success.

What Recruiters Look For

Recruiters understand that you will not be able to answer every question perfectly, and they also understand that you may not know the answer to each question that is asked. What they do expect and what they are interested in is how you respond to certain lines of questioning and how you conduct yourself. As such, their line of questioning will be designed to reveal your ability to:

✦ Listen actively
✦ Express yourself articulately, confidently and professionally
✦ Answer questions logically and concisely
✦ Remain calm under pressure

Some of the questions are designed specifically to throw you off guard, to see how you react to the pressure. With these sorts of questions, the interviewers are not necessarily looking for a perfect answer, but they are looking for a quick and well-prepared response.

Ultimately, it is important to remember that the recruiters are looking to hire positive people, so it is important to remain calm and composed throughout the interview and never show that you have been flustered.

Avoid Flat Answers

While it may make sense to memorise your answers, I would advise against this. Not only do you run the risk of sounding like a robot, with a boring and flat delivery, but you also risk forgetting your answers and appearing flustered as you try to recall the information.

Rather than memorising your answers, make a list of key points and try to remember those instead. Key points are much easier to remember and will allow you to create a genuine and spontaneous answer based around those key points.

Another technique, that is highly effective and advantageous, is to prepare through actual practice. Whether that is through a role play with a friend or family member, the use of a camcorder or through attending mock interviews with other airlines, practice will allow you to feel much more con dent and natural when you do the real thing.

And remember to inject your personality as much as possible. Have stories at the ready and personal anecdotes because that is what will make you stand out and likeable, but also make you believable in your response.

Where people get lost is in not preparing at all and winging it, or over preparing and appearing static in their delivery. Take the middle ground. Just be yourself and be natural following the structures provided.

Anticipate Questions

Your résumé is a very powerful document because it will influence the nature and direction of the interview to a great extent. The recruiters have no information about you beyond this piece of paper, so they will use it to formulate suitable questions. This allows an element of predictability, therefore giving you back some control.

Take a look through your resume and consider what questions may arise from what you have included. For example:

✈ If you have been self employed for some time, this could pose concerns about your ability to return to employment
✈ If you have large gaps in your employment or are currently unemployed, what are the reasons for those?
✈ Do you have only a short career history? or maybe you are going through a big career change, for what reason have you decided to change career paths?

Also take time to consider questions what may be relevant speci cally to the airline or the position

✈ If the position involves a relocation, you may be asked about your knowledge of the location being transferred to.
✈ If there is a cultural element, you may be asked questions about your knowledge there also.
✈ And what about the challenges of the position. You'll most certainly want to know how you'll cope with the demands of the job
You don't need to have a solid answer for every single thing, but you should give some thought to anything that is obvious.

When I was being interviewed for Emirates, I was asked about my knowledge of Dubai and how I would cope with the transition to living within a Muslim country.

My history of self employment was brought up as a concern, as was my willingness to relocate to Dubai. They even asked if I would miss my family and how I would feel to miss out on special family occasions.

Think ahead.

TRADITIONAL
QUESTIONS

Traditional Questions As Easy as A.B.C

When preparing your answers to traditional questions, keep the A.B.C formula in mind.

A - Answer
Make your answer concise by answering the question directly

B - Back it up
Back up your answer with solid facts. This will add a lot of weight to any statements made.

C - Conclude
The conclusion allows you to expand on your skills and what you can offer the airline

Consider the following example:

Example: What is your best attribute?

ANSWER
"As you will have observed during the group assessments, I am a very welcoming and social individual who interacts well with others, and readily adapts to new people and environments."

BACK IT UP
"In fact, my previous supervisor also picked up on these attributes and often asked me to carry out the client shampoo because she knew I would make the clients feel welcome and relaxed"

CONCLUDE
"I am con dent that this aspect of my character will enable me to perform the job to the same high standard that exists currently within the airline"
Traditional Questions

A.C.T on Negative Questions

Negative questions can be better approached using the A.C.T formula

A - Attack
By attacking the question head on, not only do you avoid being alienated by the question, it also allows you to swiftly move on and add clarity to your response.

C - Clarify
This is your opportunity to add any clarity and facts that may support or justify your answer.

T - Turn
Now turn the focus away from the initial negative question to focus on the positive outcome of the experience.

Consider the following example:

Example: What do you consider to be your greatest weakness?

ATTACK
"I recognise that my leadership ability is a potential area of improvement"

CLARIFY
"Which is why I am actively working on developing this area further through a part time training course at my local college"

TURN
"Although I am still learning, I see constant improvement in my capabilities when being faced with leadership tasks and I am con dent that I will continue to learn and grow with experience"

Probing Questions

Follow up questions are either used to verity the viability of your answer, or to tempt negative information into the open. So it is important to have examples ready to back up any statements made.

Prepare to be asked:

➤ What did you learn from the experience?
➤ What specifically did you say?
➤ How did you feel?
➤ Would you do anything differently?
➤ How did they react?
➤ What other options did you consider?
➤ Why did you decide to take the action that you did?
➤ You mentioned ... Tell me more about that.
➤ How did you retain your composure?
➤ Can you give me an example of that?
➤ Can you be more specifics about...?

Sample answers for the top 10 traditional questions

Tell me a little bit about yourself

This question is usually asked early as an ice breaker. There is no need to delve into your childhood leisure pursuits here, the recruiters simply want a paraphrased overview of what you do, why you are attending the interview and what you have to offer. Show your personality because they want to learn more about you as a person, not simply a rehash of your resume.

"I currently work as a freelance hair consultant, and have worked in client-facing roles for the past eight years. During this time, I have worked my way up from a receptionist to a senior hair stylist, while simultaneously studying for my NVQ levels 1, 2 and 3.

While I very much enjoy the work I do, I'd love the chance to transfer the skills and experiences I have learnt to work as cabin crew, which is why I'm so excited about this opportunity with Emirates Airlines.

Even back as far as being a child, I have always wanted to become cabin crew and, during the course of my career, I have been gradually mastering the skills needed to perform its tasks. I'd now like to discuss how I might contribute to the ongoing success of Emirates Airlines by joining your team."

Why do you want to become cabin crew?

An honest and passionate response to this question will surely set you apart. Think about it, why do you really want the job? Where did the desire come from? Was it a childhood dream, or was it sparked by another interest? Let your personality shine.

"For me, it's not just the job, but the whole lifestyle that interests me. On a personal note, I love the buzz of the airport because to me it represents action. The sense of satisfaction that everyone has a story and everyone is going somewhere for a reason sets off the excitement and motivation in me.

On a professional note, however, being a representative of the Emirates brand and being a part of the aviation industry are factors which draw me. Just being in the thick of things, in amongst the passengers where I can contribute to their entire experience is a major draw.

But ultimately, I want the job because I know I will be good at it. Not only would I positively thrive on the challenges of the position, but I have also built up a solid set of skills that will enable me to truly excel within the role.

Being cabin crew with Emirates Airlines really encapsulates everything that I want in a long term career and I can't think of anything I'd rather do."

Why do you want to work for Emirates?

"Well, it actually goes back to my very first flight. I was finally earning enough to take my dream trip to Singapore and chose to fly with Emirates. Once on board, your crew did everything to make my flight the most memorable experience, and it has never been matched.

Once they had completed their crew duties, two of the crew offered to take me for a tour around the aircraft and into the flight deck to meet the pilots. Later into the flight, I had fallen asleep and missed the meals, but woke from my nap to find my tray table down and there were 3 chocolates on top of a hand written note which read "from your Emirates crew".Clearly this isn't part of the job description, so I was really impressed with the extra effort they had extended to me on my maiden voyage.

With this as a first experience, the bar has been set high and I've not encountered any experience like it, neither have I met such a dedicated and enthusiastic crew. I have also met many more Emirates crew who have worked for the airline for several years and still speak lovingly about their job and the airline. This, to me, is a clear testament of the Emirates brand and the quality of training you provide.

I would be honoured to work for and represent the Emirates brand and pass on that same smile I was awarded to another passenger."

What do you know about Emirates?

This is where your research will pay off handsomely. So, demonstrate your enthusiasm by sharing knowledge that will reveal the effort you have taken to learn more about the airline and its operations.

"Emirates Airlines began operating on the 25th October 1985. The airline now serves 155 destinations, in 82 countries and across 6 continents. and is rapidly expanding its route network with Phnom Penh in Cambodia being it's newest route.

From my personal experience of being a passenger, I also discovered that the Best Airline in the World award given by TripAdvisor Travellers Choice Awards 2017 is certainly deserved as I have always found the most welcoming and enthusiastic crew on board my flights with Emirates Airlines.

I also note during my research that Emirates have a rapidly expanding fleet of aircraft, with the largest aircraft deals and largest fleet of A380's."

What qualities do you think are necessary for cabin crew?

The recruiters want to know that you understand what the role involves and what qualities are necessary to perform its tasks. Conclude this answer by acknowledging your skills in relation to the position.

"Cabin crew play a vital role in giving a good impression of the airline as a whole. This means crew members need to have good communication and customer care skills, as well as a friendly and welcoming demeanour, at all times and without exception.

Because of the importance of safety, it is also important that they have the strength of character to cope with difficult people and situations, in a calm and objective manner. It is also important that crew are respected as an authority if they are to be listened to and taken seriously, so an inner confidence, a sense of leadership and ability to be assertive are also essential skills.

Incidentally, these are all attributes I have, and are the primary reasons I would complement your existing team."

What are your best qualities?

Don't be shy, give it all you got. But, be sure to back it up with examples, ideally one which relates to the position if you have one.

ANSWER
This is a tough one to answer, but I'm going to say enthusiasm. Whatever happens in my life and no matter how bad things get, I am always able to see the positive aspects and keep a calm head. I think this has come from all the Tony Robbins videos I have watched.

BACK IT UP
I remember during my degree, I used to post little pep talk messages on the private group forum whenever I felt excited. The more I was struggling with an aspect of the course, the more positive and frequent my messages became. Often I would have a message from another student telling me how my message had come at the right time and it had put a smile on their face.

CONCLUDE
Not only does it help me remain positive and focused, but I get a huge sense of satisfaction when I am able to impart that enthusiasm onto others.

What is your greatest weakness?

The key to answering questions about weaknesses is to focus your response on those skills you are actively learning or planning to develop. This could be assertiveness or leadership. The point is, it is only a weakness because you haven't yet mastered it, and that is why you are working on developing those skills further. Avoid weaknesses that are an integral part of the position.

ANSWER
Well, such is the joy of life, my greatest strength is also my greatest weakness. In being enthusiastic, I have learnt that not everyone is in tune or on that same level and doesn't necessarily want to be.

BACK IT UP
I am learning to develop my awareness skills to understand when my enthusiasm is appropriate, and when it needs to be reigned in slightly.

CONCLUDE
It's taking some conscious effort to reign myself in, and I'm at the stage where my brain feels fried, but I'm getting better the more I practice, and I'm receiving positive feedback. I'm con dent that I can get those skills where I need them to be and I see it as a good opportunity to develop my people sills further.

Why should we hire you?

This is the time to shine, so don't be modest. Consider the experience and character traits that are most relevant and transferable to the position and explain how you have demonstrated these in the past.

ANSWER
"Honestly, I feel as thought this job description was written with me in mind. I have worked in client facing roles for the past eight years so I am certainly qualified to perform the diverse requirements of this role but, beyond this, my character is tailored to this role.

BACK IT UP
As you will have observed during the group assessments, I am a very welcoming and social individual who interacts well with others. I readily adapt to new people and environments and I can work alongside others as part of a unified team.

CONCLUDE
These are all skills and qualities I will bring to the position and I am con dent that these aspects of my personality and experience will enable me to perform the job to the same high standard that exists currently."

Why did you leave your last job?

While you do need to be honest about your reasons for leaving past employment, you need to be diplomatic in your response. Being bored or not getting along with your boss are not ideal answers here

No Opportunties
"While I enjoyed working for my previous employer, and appreciate the skills I developed while I was there, I felt I was not being challenged enough in the job. After working my way up through the company, there were no further opportunities for advancement."

Redundancy
"I survived the first layoffs, but unfortunately this one got me."

Temporary Position
"The job was only a temporary position which I took to broaden my experience."

What do you dislike about your current job?

There will always be less than exciting aspects of a job, however, being critical about your job isn't going to create a positive impression. So, soften these aspects as much as possible and try to select neutral examples, such as paperwork, lack of job security or opportunities for growth.

"I honestly can't think of any major dislikes. I don't think I'd be able to really excel if I weren't truly interested in the work, or if I were merely motivated by its financial rewards. I guess my answer will have to come under the category of nuisances.

The biggest nuisance is the paperwork. I realise the importance of documentation, and I cooperatively ll out the forms, but I'm always looking for efficiencies in that area that will get me out in front of the client where I belong."

BEHAVIOURAL
QUESTIONS

The majority of this questioning will focus almost exclusively on personal qualities and behavioural questions. With this type of questioning there are no right or wrong answers, just more appropriate answers and better forms of expression.

The reason for this style of interview is because how you have applied certain skills and behaved in the past is often a clear indication of how you will behave in the future. In essence, the interviewers are looking to predict your future performance and determine if you have the qualities required to perform the duties of the role.

The key to preparing for this type of interview is to work with the job description and person specification that we covered in step one. All you need to do is tailor your answers to match and demonstrate those competencies.

Because you won't know what questions will be asked, it is important to enter the process with 3-5 short stories that highlight the most important core competencies. At the bare minimum, try to have an example for each of the following

✈ Team Spirit
✈ Customer Service
✈ Communication
✈ Challenging Experience

You can expect questions to similar to the following:

✈ Tell us about a time when you went out of your way to help a customer
✈ When could your customer service have been better?
✈ When have you solved a customer problem?
✈ Have you been confronted by an angry customer before?
✈ Tell me about a time when you have worked well within a team
✈ Have you ever struggled to t in with your team mates?
✈ Tell me about a disagreement you have had with your colleagues
✈ Tell me about a problem you have faced and the steps you took to overcome it.

The S.A.R.R Formula

When preparing your examples to competency-based questions, the S.A.R.R formula can help you structure your response.

S - Situation
Briefly describe the challenge, problem, or task

A - Action
Describe what you did and how you did it

R - Result
Describe the outcome and how your actions affected the outcome or the people involved

R - Reflection
Elaborate on what you learned from the experience and whether you would do things differently in the future.

Consider the following example:

Example: When have you used your initiative to solve a problem?

SITUATION
"I was in the staff room during my lunch break, and I could hear a lot of noise coming from inside the salon. I went to investigate and two, very bored, little girls confronted me. I could sense that their excitement was causing a disruption and inconvenience"

ACTION
"I immediately took the initiative and attempted to occupy them by offering to plait their hair while they made bracelets from some hair beads. Their eyes sparkled with excitement and I was able to keep them occupied for the remainder of their visit"

RESULT
"We had lots of fun and, while the calm was restored, the stylist was able to complete their mothers' treatment"

REFLECTION
"I felt really pleased that with just a little extra effort, I had made such a big difference"

Sample answers for behavioural questions

When have you gone out of your way for a customer?

Example 1

Situation:
I had a client call into the store who was looking for a very specific style of fabric. She had visited several stores in and around the area but hadn't been successful in her search. I could see that she was exhausted, but also very determined. She spoke with such sorrow in her voice that I actually began to feel sorry for the poor lady because I didn't have the fabric to sell her.

Action:
Not wanting to be the bearer of more bad news, I decided to offer my assistance. I spent several hours ringing around wholesalers, distributors and manufacturers trying to track down this particular fabric, when finally I struck gold with a small manufacturing plant.

Result:
Because the fabric was a special order, there was a small handling charge, but the customer received the fabric within a few days and was sure it was worth the expense and wait.

Example 2

Situation:
I encountered a problem when one of my clients was unable to have a hair treatment carried out in her home because it was being renovated.

Action:
In an attempt to keep the client, I spoke to a contact I had within a local salon and was able to negotiate a small fee for use of the salon facilities.

Result:
This worked out really well because it was convenient for both myself and the client to travel to. Since then, I have negotiated similar deals with four other salons and have increased my customer base dramatically as a direct result.

Describe a time when your customer service could have been better?

Providing excellent customer service is vital, so you should be very cautious when providing negative examples.

You could take a modest approach and explain that you always strive to do better, or you could be honest with humble example.

Alternatively, you could attempt to avoid providing an example by explaining how you maintain your standards, and then proceed with an example of a time when you have demonstrated this capability.

Modest Approach
I take great pride in providing the best service I possibly can, but in doing so I increase my skills and can always see room for improvement.

No Experience
I take great pride in providing the best service I possibly can, and I never let my standards slip. Even during times of high pressure, I make an effort to remain courteous and helpful. I can honestly say that I have never received any negative feedback.

When have you solved a customer problem?

Situation:
I remember a client who came to me to have her hair extensions replaced. She had worn sewn in extensions for several months and was experiencing some discomfort from the attachments.

Action:
As I examined her hair, I was shocked to discover how much damage had been caused. Her roots had become severely matted and the tightness from the installed tracks had created spots of baldness.

I took a moment to analyse the situation, work out a strategy and then I set to work.

I spent several hours meticulously untangling every hair and removing every extension piece, The more I removed, the more I could see the scale of the damage that had been caused. Sadly, the client's hair was in very bad shape after the removal and the spots of baldness were very evident. Needless to say, I had a very emotional customer.

I applied a very deep conditioning protein treatment to the customers remaining locks and gave it a good trim. I then finished up with some fine and strategically placed fusion hair extensions to conceal the bald patches and create some much needed volume.

Result:
Following the treatment, the client looked fantastic and her smile was restored. Her hair soon returned to its former glory and she became a regular client of mine.

When have you tended to an upset customer?

Situation:
I recently experienced a situation with a client who was having relationship problems. She was becoming increasingly emotional and I could sense that she was feeling very depressed.

Action:
Although I felt compassion for her situation, I knew that it was important for me not to get overly involved. So, I gave her chance to talk while I listened, and I tried to show empathy while remaining neutral and professional in my response.

Result:
Just being able to talk to someone who listened seemed to make her feel better. As she continued to speak, she appeared to have gained a deeper insight into her situation and actually began seeing things more positively. Consequently, she was able to calmly discuss her feelings with her partner and work through their problems. She later thanked me for listening.

Reflection:
From this experience, I learned that just listening can be providing good customer care.

Have you been confronted by an aggressive customer?

Situation:
Shortly after I began freelancing, I encountered a problem when an associate of mine tried to pressure me into a free service based on friendship.

Action:
I proceeded to offer her, what I considered to be, a reasonable discount, but she was not satisfied with my offer and proceeded to pressure me with emotional blackmail. I remained cordial, but became more assertive as I continued to refuse her demands.

Result:
Rather than accept the reasons for my decision, she became increasingly enraged, and even began to slander my service and friendship .

Shocked at her over-reaction, and concerned about what might develop, I felt I had no option but to withdraw from the situation.

Reflection:
This experience was very challenging and certainly tested my patience. But I remained calm and, although this particular relationship never recovered, it was a learning experience that hasn't since been repeated.

When have you had to say 'No' to a customer?

There will be occasions when it is necessary to say no to a passenger. The recruiter wants to know that you aren't intimidated by such situations and have the strength of character to deal with the situation authoritatively, yet diplomatically.

You will be assessed on how you approached the customer and went about dealing with the situation. A good response will demonstrate your ability to use tact, and will show that you remained courteous throughout the experience.

Situation:
I remember when a customer tried to return a pair of trainers to the store for a refund. Although the customer denied it, I could see that the shoes had clearly been worn.

Action:
I remained calm and polite as I suggested that the shoes could not be returned unless faulty or unused.

The customer become very aggressive and repeatedly threatened to contact our head office to complain about me if I didn't refund him immediately.

I remained assertive and suggested this would be the best course of action for him to take. I then proceeded to provide him with the full details of our complaints manager within the head office.

Result:
Realising defeat, the man stormed out of the shop and, to my knowledge, never did take the matter further.

When have you handled a customer complaint?

Situation:
I remember when a customer complained about a meal they had purchased.

Because over two thirds of the entire course had been eaten, not only was it obvious that the complaint was insincere, but it was also against the restaurants policy to offer a refund under such circumstances.

The customer was becoming very enraged and threatened to write to the trading standards and newspapers if I did not give him a full refund.

Action:
I gave the customer my undivided attention while he vented his frustrations. Then, when he had finally calmed down, I calmly apologised for the dissatisfaction and proceeded to offer a meal deal voucher as a goodwill gesture.

Result:
The customer was clearly unhappy not to have received a refund, but he left the restaurant and, as suspected, never did take the matter any further.

When have you had to resolve a conflict between what the customer wanted and what you could realistically deliver?

Situation:
I remember a client who came to me for a colour treatment and restyle. She had used a virtual hairstyle software to create her ideal look and was beaming with excitement as she showed me the picture.

The style was notably very pretty, and it was clear that it was ideally suited to the client. Unfortunately, however, the client's hair had been through several perming and colour treatments, and the platinum blonde shade that she wanted just wasn't going to be possible at that time.

Action:
Knowing how excited the client was, I felt a little dejected as I proceeded to break this news to her. In the hope of relieving some of her obvious disappointment, I suggested a strand test to see if it would be possible to lift some of the colour without causing excessive damage. If the strand test were a success, we could perform a gradual transformation through the use of highlights.

Result:
Thankfully, the strand test was a success and the client, while naturally disappointed, was happy to go ahead with the gradual transformation. The result was striking, and the client was happy with the result.

Within nine months, the transformation was complete, and I had a very satisfied customer.

Describe a situation when the customer was wrong

Although the popular saying suggests otherwise, the customer isn't always right and the recruiter wants to know that you aren't Intimidated by such situations.

You will be assessed on how you approached the customer and went about dealing the situation. A good response will demonstrate your ability to use tact, and will show that you remained courteous throughout the experience.

Situation:
I remember a client who I had carried out a perming treatment for. After completing the treatment, I provided written instructions for how to care for her new perm which specifically instructed against washing the hair for at least 48 hours.

Unfortunately, the very next day the client washed her hair and the perm dropped out. The client was understandably very upset, but refused to accept that the perm had fallen out as a consequence of her own actions. She became very irate and started to slander my work and the salon.

Action:
When asked if she had followed the instructions, she denied being provided with any. I assured her that instructions were provided, and suggested she check her belongings.

Result:
Later that afternoon, the client returned to the salon holding onto the instruction sheet with a very embarrassed look on her face. She apologised profusely for her behaviour. Reflection: To avoid a repeat of this situation, I now provide clearer warnings within the written information sheet and back it up with verbal instructions.

Have you ever bent the rules for a customer?

There are situations where it is permissible to bend the rules, however, airlines may view rule bending very negatively. So, no matter how trivial or well-intended, you may want to play it safe and declare that you have never gone against the rules.

If you do decide to provide an answer, you should show that you are able to keep balance between company policy and the interest of customers.

I have always abided by company policies and have never bent the rules. Bending the rules for one customer, will no doubt lead to a downward spiral . Either the customer will expect further rule bending, or other customers will catch on and expect the same treatment. It's just not a wise course of action to take.

Tell me about a time when you failed to communicate effectively?

We all experience challenges in communication, but a complete failure to communicate effectively will show a lack of initiative and creativity in problem solving.

Whatever the reason for a communication challenge, there is always a way to communicate if you are willing to put in some additional effort. Your answer should reflect this.

Modest Response
While I have certainly encountered communication challenges, I can honestly say that I have never yet completely failed in my ability to communicate. With some creativity, I have always found a way to overcome communication barriers.

Humble Response
Situation:
Generally, I am a very efficient communicator, but I do recall when I experienced difficulty communicating with an OAP client.

Action:
The client was very hard of hearing, and I tried everything to communicate with her. I spoke slower, louder, used hand gestures and facial expressions, I even tried to write the information down, but without her glasses she was unable see my writing clearly.

Result:
Fortunately, I managed to locate a magnifying glass, which enabled the client to read my instructions, and everything worked out well in the end.

When have your communication skills made a difference to a situation or outcome?

> The ability to communicate well is vital to the role of cabin crew, so you should have plenty of real life examples ready to share. This is your chance to shine, so don't be modest.

Situation:
I remember a trainee apprentice we had in our department who never asked questions and refused all offers of help. Unfortunately, instead of trying to understand her reasons, everyone drew the conclusion that she was a know-it-all and vowed not to offer help in the future.

Action:
Concerned that her progress would suffer, I decided to offer my encouragement and support. It soon became evident from our conversation that she had excessively high expectations of herself and feared looking incompetent. I explained that it was okay to ask questions, and mistakes were expected. I even shared a few of my own early mishaps to lighten the mood.

Result:
Very quickly after that we saw a change in her behaviour. She began asking questions, she was more open to suggestions, and her skills improved immensely.

Reflection:
From this experience, I learnt that things are not always what they appear and we need to be more objective before making rash judgements.

Give an example of when you had to present complex information in a simplified manner in order to explain it to others

As cabin crew, you may be required to break down and convey complex information to customers. For example, if a passenger is afraid of flying, you may need to explain the technicalities of the flight, or if a passenger is hasn't grasped the use of emergency equipment and emergency procedures, you may need to break the information down further.

Your answer here should show that you are able to express knowledge in a clear and simple manner.

Situation:
I remember a client who was interested in having a colour treatment carried out. She was very inquisitive and asked numerous questions, so I could sense that she was concerned about the process and potential damage to her natural hair.

Action:
Not satisfied with a simple nontechnical version, I had to provide a detailed technical breakdown of the whole process. This involved describing the molecular structure of the hair, the effect colour particles have and how they bond to the structure.

Result:
Although I had to occasionally refer to training manuals to emphasise or clarify my point, overall the client was satisfied with my effort. As a direct result, she went ahead with the treatment and was very pleased with the outcome.

Have you ever had to overcome a language barrier?

As cabin crew, you will interact with a variety of people from a broad range of cultures and backgrounds. The ability to relate to others and adapt your communication style is, therefore, very important.

Situation:
During a trip to Africa, I became acquainted with a French lady. She understood my French, the little amount I knew, but she didn't really understand English. Unfortunately, the amount of French I knew wasn't enough to get me through a whole conversation, so I had to improvise.

Action:
I spoke French wherever possible and filled in the gaps with improvised sign language and facial expressions.

Result:
At first it was a little tricky trying to find imaginative ways to communicate, but over time I became much more proficient. I'm sure she was amused by my amateur efforts, but it worked out well and I came away with a new friend.

Reflection:
Now when I encounter this type of communication barrier, I am much more confident in my ability to cope.

Tell me about a time that you had to work as part of a team

> The ability to work well within a team is absolutely essential to working as cabin crew. You should, therefore, have plenty of examples that demonstrate this ability.

Situation:
There was a particular time that stands out for me because it was such an unusual occurrence.

It was a usual quiet Tuesday afternoon and only myself, the senior stylist, an apprentice, and the salon manager were on duty. To our surprise, it was as if someone started offering out free chocolate, as clients started to filter through the doors.

Action:
Despite the overwhelming rush, we showed great teamwork as we pulled together and shared our duties. Even our manager showed great team spirit as she got involved with the hair service.

Result:
As a result of our teamwork, and some free relaxing conditioning treatments, we managed to deliver an outstanding service. Every client went away completely satisfied.

When have you struggled to fit in?

> With the constant rotation of crew, there will be some people that you don't immediately hit it off with. The recruiters want to know that you aren't intimidated by such difficulties and are able to move past any struggles.

Situation:
When I started working at Trina's Hair & Beauty, I was joining a very close-knit team who had been together for a number of years.

As a result of the number of trainees they had witnessed come and go over the years, they had become a little reluctant to accept new trainees.

I wouldn't say it was a struggle to fit in as such, but I certainly experienced some growing pains. With remarks such as 'if you are still here then' to contend with, I knew I had to prove myself.

Action:
To show that I was serious about the job, and was not a fly-by-night, I focused a lot of effort on learning my new job. At the same time, I continued to be friendly and respectful of my new colleagues while I made a conscious effort to get to know them.

Result:
As a result of my hard effort, It didn't take long for them to accept me and include me as part of their team. Naturally, I have become closer to some of my colleagues than with others, but we all got on and worked well as a team.

Have you ever experienced difficulties getting along with colleagues?

No matter how hard we try, or how likeable we are, there will always be someone that we don't hit it off with. To say otherwise, would not sound credible.

For the most part, this question is asked to determine your ability to get along with other people and manage adversity. The recruiters want to know that you don't allow conflict to interfere with work.

The best answer should show that you aren't intimidated or confrontational in such situations, but you put in the commitment necessary to build a respectful and healthy working relationship.

Situation:
I remember one co-worker in particular who flat out didn't like me. It didn't matter what I did or said, or whether I tried to avoid or befriend this person.

Action:
After a couple of days of subtle hostility, I decided to assert myself. I diplomatically explained that I acknowledged her dislike for me and I asked for input as to what I must do to create a professional relationship.

Result:
Although we never became friends, we were able to maintain more cordial relations thereafter.

Tell us about a challenge you have faced with a colleague

Airlines have a constant rotation of crew on-board each aircraft and, especially within larger airlines, you may not work with the same crew members twice. As a result, it is guaranteed that you will encounter challenging situations with colleagues.

The recruiters want to know that you aren't intimidated by such colleagues or situations, and are prepared to use your initiative to diffuse or mediate as necessary to keep working relationships healthy.

Your answer should demonstrate your willingness to cooperate with others to resolve differences, improve relations, and manage conflicts. It should also display your ability to remain patient and positive in the face of adversity.

Situation:
I do remember one situation where two of my colleagues really didn't hit it off with one another. They were constantly quarrelling and everyone had lost patience with them, but no one wanted to get involved.

Action:
In the end, I decided to take the initiative and act as a sort of mediator to the situation. I was not their manager, so I had to be as tactful as I could so that I wouldn't upset anyone.

I started by explaining that I acknowledged their dislike for each other and then I drew upon the fact that they are both professionals and can, therefore, put aside their differences for the good of the team.

Result:
They had a pretty frank discussion and, although I can't say they ended up the best of friends, they did work out an effective strategy for working more productively together.

Tell me about a disagreement with a colleague

We all have disagreements with colleagues, but they should never get out of control or interfere with work.

You may choose to disclose the details of a conflict situation, but make sure it was minor and didn't interfere with work. Conversely, you may wish to play it safe and declare that while you have had disagreements, they were so minor that you don't really recall the exact details. You could then go on to reiterate some minor examples.

The recruiters want to know that you aren't intimidated by conflicts and have the ability to see things from another person's perspective. Your answer should demonstrate that you are prepared to use your initiative and interpersonal skills to improve relations with colleagues, even in cases where they cannot agree upon certain issues.

Introduction:
Working in a creative environment with other highly skilled professionals, it was natural that we had the occasional clash of ideas. Any disagreements we did have, however, were so relatively minor and insignificant that I would be hard pressed to recall the exact details.

Situation:
Our disagreements were usually as a result of our individual preference towards certain products, styles, magazines or equipment.

Action:
Our debates were never confrontational and they never interfered with our work in any way.

Result:
In fact, some very interesting views emerged from these debates which sometimes resulted in people, including myself, having a slight change in my perspective. So, they were often very educational.

Have you successfully worked with a difficult coworker?

The recruiters want to know that you aren't intimidated by difficult colleagues or situations, and are prepared to use your initiative to deal with the situation as necessary. You will be assessed on how you approached the colleague and how you dealt with the situation.

Your answer should demonstrate your willingness to co-operate with others to resolve differences, improve relations, and manage conflicts. It should also display your ability to remain patient and positive when challenging situations occur.

Situation:
I remember one member of staff was always complaining. Nothing was ever good enough or couldn't possibly work. Everyone had lost patience with her but, because she was so incredibly sensitive, no one said anything.

Action:
I spent some time with her and tactfully told her that it appeared as if she was always putting our ideas down.

Result:
On hearing this feedback she was genuinely horrified at her own behaviour. She explained that she hadn't realised it had made everyone feel that way and agreed that from then on she would try to be more positive.

Very quickly after that we saw a change in her behaviour. She became more conscious of her own attitude and deliberately tried to be more considerate. From that point on, no one could have hoped for a more committed team member.

Have you ever worked with someone you disliked?

There will always be someone that we don't like and to try to convince the recruiter otherwise would not sound honest or credible.

For the most part, this question is asked to determine your ability to get along with other people and manage adversity. The recruiters want to know that you don't allow personal views cause conflict or interfere with work.

The best answer should show that you aren't intimidated or confrontational in such situations, but you put in the commitment necessary to build a respectful and healthy working relationship

Situation:
There was one colleague I worked with that I really found it difficult to get along with personally.

Action:
Instead of focusing on those things I didn't like, I put my personal views aside and focused on the skills she brought to the position.

Result:
My personal view of her never changed, and we never became friends, but we did work productively alongside each other without any problems.

Have you ever acted as a mentor to a coworker?

There may be times when you have to mentor new crew members and the recruiters are trying to assess your ability to lead and mentor your colleagues.

Situation:
I remember when one of our trainees was having problems understanding certain aspects of her course material, and I could see she was becoming increasingly frustrated and self critical.

Action:
Having witnessed her in action, I knew that she was a very bright and talented individual with no obvious lack of skill. So, I determined that her frustrations were probably the result of the pressure she was feeling about her approaching exam.

Concerned at the effect this pressure was having on her, and having experienced the same pressures myself, I decided to offer my support. To reinforce her understanding, I demonstrated some of the techniques she had been struggling with and showed her a few memory tips and tricks which had helped me through my exams.

Result:
My breakdown of the processes, along with the visual demonstration I provided, seemed to make the material much more understandable for her. In the days that followed, she seemed to have a new lease of life and was much more positive. Subsequently, she passed her exams with top grades.

What have you done that shows initiative?

Situation:
When I began working for my current employer, the inventory system was outdated and the storage room was very messy and disorganised.

Action:
I came in on my day off, cleaned up the mess, organised the store cupboards and catalogued it all on the new inventory forms.

Result:
Thereafter, when orders arrived it was easy to organise and retrieve.
Reflection: If I'm able to do the task, instead of waiting for the job to be done, I simply do it.

Have you undertaken a course of study, on your own initiative, in order to improve your work performance?

Situation:
While at Trina's Hair Salon, we were experiencing a spectacular rise in demand for high fashion cuts. I had some creative cutting experience, but nothing that extended to the kind of advanced skill that was required for true high fashion cuts.

Action:
After some consideration, I decided that increasing my creative cutting skills would not only give the salon a competitive advantage, but it would also be a fantastic opportunity for me to move my skills to the next level. So, I took the initiative and, under my own funding, immediately enrolled onto a creative cutting course.

Result:
My new skills proved to be an instant success. Existing clients began recommending me to their friends, which resulted in a massive rise in clientele. Needless to say, my manager was very happy.

Describe an improvement that you personally initiated\

> The recruiter wants to know that you seek better and more effective ways of carrying out your work and can suggest improvements that will achieve more efficiency. Your answer here should show that you take the initiative when it comes to improving working methods and standards.

Situation:
While travelling in India, I learnt the art of Indian head massage.

Action:
When I returned to work, I began using my new skill on clients while carrying out the shampoo.

Result:
My massages were becoming such a success, that my manager approached me to request that I train my colleagues. Naturally, I was honoured to oblige.

Describe a new idea or suggestion that you made to your supervisor

> The recruiter wants to know that you aren't afraid to take the initiative and suggest improvements.

Situation:
When I was working at Trina's Hair Salon, I had noticed that a lot of our clients wore nail extensions.

Action:
Convinced that the service would be an improvement to our already successful salon, I carried out extensive independent research before presenting the idea to my manager.

Result:
After carrying out her own research, she liked the idea so much that she decided to go ahead with the new service. Within a couple of months, the service was up and running, and we experienced a dramatic increase in new clientele and revenue. I even got a small bonus in my pay packet for my involvement.

Tell me about a problem you encountered and the steps you took to overcome it

The recruiter will be assessing how well you cope with diverse situations, and how you use your judgment and initiative to solve problems.

In answering this question, you need to provide a concrete example of a problem you faced, and then Itemize the steps you took to solve the problem. Your answer should demonstrate a patient and positive attitude towards problem solving.

Situation:
Early in my freelancing career, I experienced several clients who turned up late to their appointments. Some even forgot about their appointments altogether. Rather than just simply being an inconvenience, it was wasting my time and money.

Action:
I considered my options and decided that the best solution would be to send out reminder cards a few days prior to client appointments. For the repeat offenders, I would enforce a late cancellation fee.

Result:
This decision drastically cut the number of late arrivers, and I have never since had a no-show.

Tell me about a problem that didn't work out

No matter how hard we try, there are some instances where a problem just doesn't work out. To say otherwise will not sound honest or credible.

In answering this question, you need to first ensure that the problem was a minor one which had no negative or lasting impact on the company, a colleague or a customer. Try to accentuate the positives and keep your answer specific. Itemize the steps you took to deal with the problem and make it clear that you learnt from the experience.

Situation:
Shortly after I began freelancing, my bank returned a client's cheque to me through lack of funds.

Action:
At first, I was sure it was a mistake caused through an oversight on the part of my client. I made a number of calls, left several messages and even attempted a visit to the clients home, all to no avail.

Several weeks passed and it was clear that I was chasing a lost cause. At this point, I had to decide whether to write off the debt and blacklist the client or visit the Citizens' Advice for advice on retrieving the funds.

Result:
After careful consideration of all the factors involved, I decided to write the debt off as a learning experience.

Reflection:
In hindsight, I realise it was a silly mistake that could easily have been avoided. I have never repeated this error since as I now wait for the funds to clear before carrying out a service.

Have you ever taken the initiative to solve a problem that was above your responsibilities?

Situation:
It had been quite an uneventful afternoon when, all of the sudden, in walked an obviously frantic customer.

From what I could understand, her laptop had contracted a virus while connected to the internet and the system now failed to respond to any commands.

Being a self-employed web designer, the customer was naturally very concerned about the potential loss of data, and earnings.

Unfortunately, while the laptop was still within warranty, it was beyond the companies scope and had to be sent to the manufacturer for restoration. My colleagues, while polite, but could only offer assistance as far as sending the laptop to the manufacturer.

Action:
I could sense the customer was becoming increasingly distressed and, having had previous training in system restoration, I was confident that I could at least safely extract the data from the hard drive.

After talking the customer through the procedure, she granted her permission and I proceeded.

Result:
After some 45 minutes of fiddling with wires and hard drives, the customer's data had been successfully, and safely, extracted. The customer gasped a big sigh of relief as we packaged the laptop off to the manufacturer for repair.

Several weeks later, my line manager received a letter from the customer complimenting my efforts.

Reflection:
I was really pleased that a little effort made such a big difference.

When have you made a bad decision?

We all make decisions that we regret, and to say otherwise will not sound honest or credible.

The recruiter will be assessing whether you have the character to admit and take responsibility for your mistake, whether your decision had a negative impact on customers or the company, and whether you learnt from this mistake?

In answering this question, you need to first ensure that the mistake was a minor one, which had no negative or lasting impact on the company, a colleague or a customer. Try to accentuate the positives and keep your answer specific. Itemize what you did and how you did it. Finally, you need to make it clear that you leant from the mistake and will be certain not to repeat it.

Situation:
Early in my freelance career, I was approached by a salesman who was promoting a protein conditioning system. He described the system as "The newest technology to emerge from years of research. Guaranteed to help heal, strengthen, and protect".

Although I was excited by the concept, I did have my concerns that the system sounded too good to be true. However, the salesman had all the official paperwork to back up his claims, and the literature was thorough and well presented. All these things, combined with the company's full money-back guarantee, made it appear to be a win-win situation, and a risk worth taking. So I invested.

Following my investment, I decided to test the system out on training heads before taking the system public. Unfortunately, several months of using the system passed with no obvious benefits.

Action:
Disappointed with the product, I decided to pursue the full money back guarantee, but the sales number was not recognised, and my letters were returned unopened. Even their website had mysteriously vanished. I soon came to the realisation that I had been taken in by an elaborate scam.

I contacted the Citizens Advice Bureau and Trading Standards, but there was little they could do to retrieve my funds.

Result:
Unfortunately, I never recovered my costs and had to put the mistake down to a learning experience.

Reflection:
Unfortunately, it really was my fault. I should have trusted my gut instinct and carried out thorough research before making my decision. It is a mistake I shall never repeat.

hat was the biggest challenge you have faced?

Situation:
To be honest, giving up smoking was the biggest challenge. I never thought I could do it, and I had made dozens of attempts that ended in failure.

Action:
Determined not to give in to my withdrawals, I decided I needed an incentive that would pull me through the tough times. Being sponsored for a worthy cause was the perfect solution.

Result:
With a good cause in mind, the following three months were easier than on previous occasions. Not only have I come out the other end a non-smoker, I also managed to raise £2464.00 for Childline.

Reflection:
Since I gave up smoking, I have gained so much personal insight, and I deal with potentially stressful situations at work so much more effectively now, I feel more energetic, more mentally alert and far calmer now than I ever did before.

QUESTIONS
FOR THE RECRUITER

This section of the interview is a real chance for you to shine and set yourself apart from all the other candidates. Therefore, it is a good idea to prepare one or two intelligent questions in advance.

The questions you ask, and how you ask them, say a lot about you, your motives, your depth of knowledge about the airline and the position itself.

Guidelines

The questions you ask should follow these guidelines:

✈ Don't ask questions that could be easily answered through your own research.
✈ Ask questions which demonstrate a genuine interest in and knowledge of the airline and the position.
✈ Demonstrate that you know just that little bit more than is required.

Questions About Suitability

Asking recruiters to raise their concerns about your suitability will provide you with an opportunity to follow up and reassure the recruiter.

✈ Do you have any reservations about my ability to do this job?
✈ What do you foresee as possible obstacles or problems I might have?
✈ Is there anything else I need to do to maximise my chances of getting this job?
✈ How does my background compare with others you have interviewed?
✈ Is there anything else you'd like to know?
✈ What do you think are my strongest assets and possible weaknesses?
✈ Do you have any concerns that I need to clear up in order to be a considered candidate?

Questions About the Recruiter

Asking recruiters about their views and experience in the job or working with the airline will demonstrate your genuine interest and motives.

✈ How did you find the transition in relocating to Dubai?
✈ How did you find the transition to living in a Muslim country?
✈ Why did you choose to work at Emirates?
✈ What is it about this airline that keeps you working here?
✈ It sounds as if you really enjoy working here, what have you enjoyed most about working for Emirates?

General Questions

✈ How would you describe the company culture?
✈ I feel my background and experience are a good t for this position, and I am very interested. What is the next step?

No Questions

✈ I did have plenty of questions, but we've covered them all during our discussions. I was particularly interested in ... but we've dealt with that thoroughly.
✈ I had many questions, but you've answered them all you have been so helpful. I'm even more excited about this opportunity than when I applied .

Questions to Avoid

You should avoid asking questions such as those following as they will make you appear selfishly motivated.

✈ How many day's holiday allowances will I receive?
✈ What is the salary?
✈ When will I receive a pay increase?
✈ How many free flights will my family receive?
✈ Can I request flights to ...?

PART FIVE
CONCLUDE

WHAT NEXT?

Emirates aim to respond within 1-2 weeks of you attending the interview/ assessment, however as recruitment is carried out globally, it normally takes around 6-8 weeks.

In the unfortunate case that you have been unsuccessful, you will receive a computer generated letter advising you of the outcome. (Please note that Emirates do not under any circumstances provide feedback with regards to the reasons).

If you are successful, you will receive an email, phone call or letter from the recruitment staff. There are various pre-joining clearances at this stage that need to be completed.

These mandatory checks include:

✈ A pre-employment medical test – to be conducted in your home country at your own expense
✈ Reference checks
✈ Joining forms - you will be advised by your assigned recruitment contact on how to access these forms.

Once the mandatory checks and supplementary steps of the process have been completed, the Human Resources Service Centre (HRSC) will make the necessary arrangements to deliver the employment contract and relevant documentation. You will also be given final clearance to resign from your current employer and subsequently, a copy of your accepted resignation may be requested.

In some cases employment contracts will be dispatched to candidates prior to the clearances being given, however the contract terms clearly state that the validity of the employment contract is subject to obtaining these pre-joining clearances. If you receive the contract prior to clearance being given, do not resign from your current employment until you are formally advised the recruitment team.

Printed by BoD˜in Norderstedt, Germany